S0-ADG-052

"In this wonderful discussion of the contours of God's loving guidance for our lives, Phil Carlson demonstrates pastoral sensitivities, theological wisdom, and an impressive grasp of the ways in which the findings of the sciences confirm revealed truths about the human condition. But most of all, he writes with a candor informed by his own deep struggles to accept an abiding, and guiding, love that can come only from the One who has created and redeemed us."

Richard J. Mouw, PhD, President and Professor of Christian Philosophy, Fuller Theological Seminary

"Dr. Carlson's book is a practical and profound reminder of the significance of our relationship with our Creator not only to our spiritual health but also to our mental and physical wellness. This book stands out from the other self-help and behavior modification books that steer clear of values and absolutes and leave us without answers. This book deals with the root causes of the behaviors that leave us depressed, anxious, overweight, and undernourished, and provides motivation to see ourselves as God sees us and to respond accordingly. Understanding who we are and what we were made to do gives clear direction in pursuing not only health but balance and purpose in our time on this earth. A well-thought-out prescription to our modern epidemic of the over-privileged and perpetually dissatisfied life, with no side effects. True integrative medicine!"

Preedar J. Oreggio, MD, Medical Director, Sierra Spring Family Wellness Center, Medical Staff Program for Torture Victims, LA

"We can find ourselves trapped in painful circumstances that look nothing like the 'good life' we dreamed we would be living. If we risk believing that change is possible, we wonder which voice to follow in a world of conflicting philosophies and advice. If you or someone you love longs to have a life worth living, *Love Written in Stone* is a trustworthy travel guide.

"Drawing on his experience as both a physician and a pastor, Dr. Carlson provides engaging stories, fresh biblical insights, and compassionate counsel. This book enables the reader to experience why the sinful and broken were drawn to Jesus, and 'the way in which He was pulling for them—longing for them to turn from the mess they had made, to choose grace, forgiveness, and a new way of life, and to find their way home.'"

Kevin and Kay Marie Brennfleck, Authors,
Live Your Calling: A Practical Guide to Finding and Fulfilling Your Mission in Life

"What matters most in life? In a beautifully written and carefully reasoned work, Phil Carlson evaluates available answers to the fundamental human quest for happiness, demonstrating the inadequacy of many of the most popular answers, and pointing us to our need to rest in the arms of the God who made us. In His caring love, God chooses to explain in His Word the remedy for so many of the problems we face in life, and these answers are carefully explained by Dr. Carlson in a way that brings encouragement and hope, reinforced by sound evidence from the sciences bearing out the positive impact of biblical wisdom.

"I admire Phil's candid openness about his own life, a reminder to all of us that the life of following Jesus is not always smooth and easy. I know few pastors with the ability to write with such intelligence, clarity, and at the same time vulnerability. I am very grateful for Phil's excellent work, and I fully recommend this book for theologians, pastors, laypeople, and anyone looking for the path to a happier and more fulfilling life."

Mihretu P. Guta, Christian Philosopher and Apologist, Author of three apologetics books in Amharic (national language of Ethiopia), Teacher at the Evangelical Theological College, Addis Ababa, Ethiopia, MA, MASR, PhD student

PHILIP CARLSON, MD

love
Written in Stone

BETHANYHOUSE
MINNEAPOLIS, MINNESOTA

Love Written in Stone
Copyright © 2011
Philip Carlson

Cover design by Lookout Design, Inc.

All emphasis in quoted Scripture is the author's.

Unless otherwise identified, Scripture quotations are from THE HOLY BIBLE, NEW INTER-
NATIONAL VERSION,® NIV® Copyright © 1973, 1978, 1984, 2010 by Biblica, Inc.™ Used by
permission. All rights reserved worldwide.

Scripture quotations identified THE MESSAGE are from *The Message*. Copyright © by Eugene H.
Peterson 1993, 1994, 1995, 1996, 2000, 2001, 2002. Used by permission of NavPress Publishing
Group.

Scripture quotations identified NLT are from the Holy Bible, New Living Translation, copyright
© 1996, 2004. Used by permission of Tyndale House Publishers, Inc., Wheaton, Illinois 60189.
All rights reserved.

All rights reserved. No part of this publication may be reproduced, stored in a retrieval system
or transmitted in any form or by any means—electronic, mechanical, photocopying, recording
or otherwise—without the prior written permission of the publisher. The only exception is brief
quotations in printed reviews.

Published by Bethany House Publishers
11400 Hampshire Avenue South
Bloomington, Minnesota 55438

Bethany House Publishers is a division of
Baker Publishing Group, Grand Rapids, Michigan.

Printed in the United States of America

Library of Congress Cataloging-in-Publication Data

Carlson, Philip M.
    Love written in stone : finding God's grace in the boundaries he sets / Philip Carlson.
        p.   cm.
    Includes bibliographical references.
    Summary: "Pastor and medical doctor looks at the laws and requirements of the Bible through
the lens of God's protective love for us"—Provided by publisher.
    ISBN 978-0-7642-0847-8 (pbk. : alk. paper) 1. Obedience—Religious aspects—Christianity.
2. Obedience—Biblical teaching.   3. God—Love.   I. Title.
    BV4647.O2C37   2011
    241'.2—dc22
                                                                            2010041254

In keeping with biblical principles of
creation stewardship, Baker Publishing Group advocates the responsible
use of our natural resources. As a
member of the Green Press Initiative,
our company uses recycled paper
when possible. The text paper of
this book is comprised of 30% post-
consumer waste.

green
press
INITIATIVE

To Carole,
whose love has helped make me whole.
Twenty-two years have seemed like a day.

PHILIP CARLSON, MD (ThM, Fuller, MD, University of Southern California) is senior pastor of Bethany Church of Sierra Madre and practices family medicine in Pasadena. His first book, *You Were Made for Love,* received a starred review from *Publishers Weekly* and was a featured selection of the Crossings Book Club. He and his wife, Carole, live in Sierra Madre, California, with their four children.

CONTENTS

INTRODUCTION

I think most of us have a hard time wrapping our heads, much more our hearts, around how much God loves us. For years I found it hard to receive love, to believe that I was loveable. I more easily felt that I was defective, awkward, unworthy, that I didn't quite measure up. God's extravagant and unrelenting love made sense for others but not for me. Several things have changed that perception over time: contemplating the gospel and Jesus' love for us expressed in his sacrifice on the cross; the reliable love of other people; and, surprisingly, the experience of being a father.

The love I experience as a father is different from any other kind of love. It's not something you fall into or grow into. It just shows up, overwhelms, and changes everything. It brings out the best in you by making you long for what is best for your child. It challenges selfishness by putting you in a position to serve, to set aside convenience. It's this crazy thing that makes you willing to die for someone you hardly know.

The day Ciara was born began such a journey. Almost four years ago, we were contacted by an adoption attorney and talked a number of times by phone with a young woman who was eighteen, pregnant, and already had two children, one of whom was in foster care. We made a commitment and began four months of waiting. Several months passed and one day we got the call. The biological mother was to be induced the next day, so Carole and I flew to Tulsa. When it was time for the delivery, we were not allowed to be in the room, but the months of waiting and the love and attachment produced in us the same feelings of excitement and concern we felt at the birth of our biological children.

But there were complications. When Ciara arrived she was in respiratory distress and rushed past us to the ICU. We waited anxiously for hours at the windows of the unit. Prematurity, a heart defect, and other issues meant she required a ventilator. As potential adoptive parents we had no status, and information was hard to come by. Finally we were allowed to see her. Carole and I sat on each side of her. There it was. That love. The same love that showed up with our other children. That crazy kind of love.

For the first few days she showed little improvement. On day four we had the added concern of a hearing in court in which a judge would make a key decision based on feedback from the biological mother that would determine the course of the adoption. We knew better than to think this was just a routine process. We had been through a failed adoption a year earlier. We were there for Aaron's birth, named him, fed him, took care of him from the day he was born. Five weeks later he left our home. The biological mother told us she needed him back because she needed the child support. We were crushed.

As we waited to hear from the social worker on the court decision about Ciara, her situation suddenly worsened. She was transferred to a nearby medical center by helicopter and we waited there in a small waiting room. We were told that it could be hours before we would be able to see her. Eight hours passed with no news. Meanwhile, the court hearing had been hours earlier, but we still hadn't heard from the social worker. Those hours of waiting were some of the most emotionally challenging hours of our lives.

Ciara's nurse finally emerged from the unit, letting us know that she was stable, but that we would not be able to see her until the next day.

We found a hotel nearby and for the next few hours I lay on my back, phone on my chest, in case a call came and in case I fell asleep.

About one thirty in the morning the phone rang. The social worker had checked her cell, heard the litany of messages. She had forgotten to call us. Describing herself as "the devil, worse than the devil," she explained that things had gone well in court and that it was just a matter of time until we would be Ciara's parents legally.

There are some things we can know through reason, the utilization of our senses, the application of scientific method. But the most basic and important questions of our existence will never be answered this way. Unless God speaks to us, unless he reveals himself, we cannot know who or what we are, the purpose or meaning of life, the depth of his care, and what he has done to reveal his love and address our needs. Unless he shows up, there are no answers.

God's Word functions to tell us that we were made by him, in his image, for relationship with him, and that he loves us with that phone-on-chest kind of love that cannot leave us ruined and helpless, that longs for our well-being and that causes him to come for us.

About a year later, I was swimming laps while having a Tevye-like conversation with God about a few things. Why the earlier failed adoption? Why all the complications surrounding Ciara's birth and her physical problems? We knew we were adopting in response to God's call, but why did it have to be so hard?

There in my friend's pool, God spoke to me, not audibly but clearly. *It sounds like you're beginning to understand just a little bit of what it means for me to be a Father.* Something shot through me. I was transfixed, almost paralyzed. I knew that God loves his children exponentially and infinitely more than I am able to love the ones he entrusts to my care. Yet I began to understand at a deeper level something qualitatively different about God's love for us, for me. It's costly. It's painful. And yet he pursues us.

God is our Father. He wants what's best for us. And he willingly does everything necessary to make it happen.

The Best Possible Life

One of the main questions always before the philosopher is simply: *What constitutes the good life?* What is the best possible way to live and how do we find our way to such a life? In the field of medicine, the question is essentially the same: How can we help people achieve health, wholeness, and happiness? I think if you asked most scientists, they'd tell you that they pursue discovery and knowledge not just for the sake of knowledge itself but with the hope of improving the human condition.

Jesus often expressed a similar concern for our well-being. "I have come that they may have life, and have it to the full" (John 10:10).

But finding our way to such a life is no simple matter.

As a family physician, my study of medicine has been rather general, and along the way I have chosen to focus time and energy on improving certain skills—things like wound closure, wound management, and the care of diabetic patients, for example. Acquiring and maintaining both the breadth and depth of knowledge to practice medicine well is a challenge. Beginning with medical school, I felt like I was drinking from a fire hydrant. But knowing how to live well is a matter far more broad, difficult, and complex than human physiology.

Both science and faith have a lot to say on the subject of lifestyle choices and quality of life. Today, science is producing a growing body of evidence supporting much of what the Christian faith has been saying all along about a way of living that leads to a better life now, what may be described as one more place where science appears to be catching up with God. One can hope that the effect of such evidence may prove to be a changed perspective on the character of God, who is often painted in one brand of contemporary literature as harsh, vindictive, or nonexistent.

God's Instructions

There are aspects to living well that are counterintuitive to us because of the effects of sin on our hearts. These effects reveal themselves in a number

12

of ways—in our lack of insight into our own motives, in our inability to connect and maintain relationships, in our blindness to our real condition, in our tendency to be guided by short-term gains without concern for long-term effects, and in our self-centeredness, to name a few.

We need help. We need direction.

This really is the point of what the Bible refers to as "law," "commandments," and "instructions." When understood in this way, we see God's commands as something more than awkward, guilt-producing, and burdensome rules. These directions for living reveal his grace and his passionate concern for our well-being. In fact, the introduction to the Psalms, the songbook of the Bible, tells us that people who do things the way God wants them done, who delight in the ways of the Lord, will be uniquely happy.

This promise of well-being has both a natural and a supernatural explanation. The natural explanation is that people doing things God's way experience positive consequences, growing and thriving "like a tree planted by streams of water" (Psalm 1:3). The supernatural explanation is simply that "the LORD watches over the way of the righteous" (Psalm 1:6), that he pays special attention to those who pay attention to him. The promise here is not the promise of an easier life, a problem-free life, but of a richer, more satisfying life.

The law and God's instruction also reveal things about our true condition. By setting a standard for a life that is beyond our own ability to achieve, the law helps us recognize our limits, our need of help, and our need for grace. We are moved away from independence and toward healthy dependence. We begin to understand some things about ourselves we did not understand before.

Think of it in terms of the importance of proper diagnosis. Christianity claims to be the answer to the human dilemma, but if we don't know what the problem is we may not recognize the answer even when we find it. Without an accurate diagnosis, we may choose to treat our condition with things that will only make it worse and in the end destroy us.

In addition to diagnosing the problem, God's instructions also function to protect us, like a guardrail on a mountain road, providing a limit, a barrier that keeps us from plunging over the edge into disaster. Apart from the guardrails and occasional warning signs, we live within a vast creation with tremendous freedom.

As people created by God, in the image of God, for relationship with God, we need his help. We need the instruction manual written by the one who designed us. John Calvin wrote, "Scripture contains the perfect rule of a good and happy life."

Evaluating the Evidence

How can we know that such claims about the kindness of God demonstrated in his instructions to us are true? And in what sense are they true? The approach to this discussion involves three parts. (1) *Examining the teachings of the Bible itself.* How does it instruct us to live? Is there any rationale provided as to why such a life is best for us? Is there any internal evidence that these guidelines might serve our best interests? (2) *Looking at the writings of some people who have done a lot of thinking* about life and the nature of things from various disciplines—theologians, philosophers, scientists, physicians, sociologists, psychologists, and others. (3) *Reviewing some of the evidence from scientific research* relevant to the ideas and themes that emerge from the Bible regarding its instructions for living.

The claims made in such a discussion are necessarily claims about the quality of life that emerges as we respond to God. Just as science cannot reveal ultimate truth about questions like who we are and life's purpose, scientific methods cannot be used to test the validity of Christianity's claims about ultimate truth. Science may be able to describe the relationship between variables like forgiveness and happiness and their impact on emotional and physical states. But science cannot tell us whether such things are ethical, moral, or virtuous.

And it is not necessarily the case that doing what God asks will always impact us positively. Discipleship is costly. Paul often described the loneliness and suffering that came with his obedience (see 2 Corinthians). And yet his losses were always accompanied by joy and contentment. Christians believe that doing what is good, virtuous, right, and meaningful, even when these choices are costly or stressful, has outweighing benefit here and now. They may not lead to health and ease, but they produce character, integrity, and hope because God can be trusted in every situation facing us. We do not do what he asks because it benefits us. We do not forgive, for example, because we might feel better about things. We forgive because we have been forgiven ourselves, because God demands it of us, and because of our desire to be like Jesus, to do what he would do if he walked in our shoes. But we are not surprised, when all is said and done, to discover the benefit.

Where are we going as we weigh these matters? What ideas shape the direction of this book?

What we find as we wander down this path is another way of telling the story of a Father's love. The story begins with love and hope but quickly turns to tragedy. The children choose a path of life characterized by self-interest, what the Bible calls "sin," which leads to the destruction of all their most important relationships—with God, others, self, and creation. The Bible is the story of what God has done to remedy this situation.

Starting down this path requires that we begin with our relationship with God and *this problem called "sin,"* because the effects of sin and loss of relationship with God are the source of all the other problems we have. As we look at what God has done to address this problem, we are faced with the importance of *forgiveness*—our need of God's forgiveness as well as the role of forgiveness in our other relationships. And returning to God—our heart's true home—produces *joy.* Joy is characteristic of children who know they are loved by their Father, bringing with it by-products like *gratitude* and *contentment,* and these characteristics transform our outlook and our approach to life.

The Bible not only addresses human reconciliation to God, but the working out of grace and reconciliation in all of our relationships. One powerful aspect of our human relationships is *our sexuality*, and the expression of our sexuality is vital because it has many potential consequences both positive and negative. Also, God's faithful, reliable love worked out in human relationships provides a context for emotional and physical health. Why does God want us to live in the context of family and community? What are *the roles of love and commitment in healthy relationships?*

The movement from connection with God to isolation impacts our relationship with ourselves as well. Some aspects of God's instructions to us regarding our own *health and wholeness* provide key pieces to the puzzle, offering a fuller understanding of God's restorative work in response to our brokenness.

We cannot fully grasp the goodness of God's instructions and directions to us without considering our *relationship with the created order.* The sheer volume of material on this subject within the Bible is impressive and for many may be surprising. This is one more place we discover that God's intentions in the project of re-creation, making all things new, are more vast and generous than anything we may have imagined.

Finally, we discover as we move along this path the unfolding of the answers to the ultimate questions of life—the ability to understand and participate in the kind of *purpose* and *meaning* found nowhere else. These things will not be learned by reading a book. They can only be recognized and realized by living out the instructions in the Book, the one our Father has written out of his concern for our well-being.

The things we will explore together in the course of this book are intended to map out a journey in which we might discover with deepening clarity more about the way God cares for us.

One note of caution: This book is not a call to law and legalism away from grace, but is instead an invitation to find tremendous grace in what God asks of us. Legalism kills. It is our effort at saving ourselves and it cannot reverse the mess we're in or remove the problems caused by sin. It gives us a false sense of control over our spiritual destiny. It can be a means of manipulation by which we guilt people into compliance. The heart of the problem with legalism is the condition of heart it produces, the failure to be for the other person. In legalism we end up comparing ourselves with others to feel morally superior to them, setting up the rules in such a way that everyone else always loses. What Jesus loathed most in legalism was this failure to be for the other person. One of the things that drew the sinful and broken to him was the way in which he was pulling for them—longing for them to turn from the mess they had made, to choose grace, forgiveness, and a new way of life, and to find their way home.

What people today refer to as religion, what Paul referred to as "works," is human effort. It is what we do to earn favor, recognition, and acceptance. On the other hand, Christianity is motivated by love and a settled recognition of God's grace, what Jesus has accomplished on our behalf.

I cannot imagine my life apart from God's grace, his revelation of himself, his choice to speak and to come to us. For someone as damaged as I am, to live with no awareness of his love, with no hope of deliverance from guilt and shame, no reasonable basis for hope in the face of death, no possible sense of purpose and meaning—for someone like me such a life would be hell.

As a parent I want the best for my kids. I pour into their lives out of the hope that they will do better than I did, avoid some of my mistakes and failures.

In my early twenties I had the privilege of being mentored by an amazing man named Mel Friesen. Mel, along with his wife, Helen, spent his entire career on the staff of InterVarsity Christian Fellowship, working with students. He had white hair, sharp features, and a fierce, unyielding devotion to Jesus. Soon before Mel went home to be with Jesus, Helen told me a story that for me captured so much about Mel's character. Their son Paul had been faced with a difficult decision in his work, and the choice he eventually made was costly and demonstrated great character. In reflecting on their son's decision, Mel said to Helen,

"He's a better man than I am." Helen told me that she replied to Mel by saying that he shouldn't say that, that she didn't know a better man than he was. Mel said, "If he's not a better man than I am, then I failed him as a father." His attitude epitomized a godly longing for the well-being of his children.

God's law and instructions demonstrate a Father's passionate concern for our well-being. His guidelines for living are not intended to cramp our style or make us miserable. They are shaped by a Father's love. They are there to point us toward the best possible life.

> This day I call heaven and earth as witnesses against you that I have set before you life and death, blessings and curses. Now choose life, so that you and your children may live and that you may love the LORD your God, listen to his voice, and hold fast to him. (Deuteronomy 30:19–20)

> The fear of the LORD is a fountain of life. (Proverbs 14:27)

PART 1:

Guidance for Our Relationship With God

one

DIAGNOSING THE PROBLEM

And the LORD God commanded the man,
"You are free to eat from any tree in the garden;
but you must not eat from the tree of the knowledge of good
and evil, for when you eat from it you will certainly die."
(GENESIS 2:16–17)

In a cave-like opening under the drooping branches of an overgrown avocado tree, a favorite hideout in my grandparents' backyard, I first sensed the world falling apart. My older brother and I were sent outside while the adults inside cried and expressed their pain in a way we had never witnessed before. My grandfather had died the night before and death left otherwise strong people wounded and confused. At age four, it felt to me like a once stable world was caving in.

When I was in college, I had to go to the home of a close friend and tell him that his father had passed away. The police had not been able to reach him, and I had somehow gotten the call. As I told Jim, we embraced, and I remember his hot tears spilling over my shoulder and an overwhelming sense of what the apostle Paul meant when he described death as an "enemy."

My friend Tamar, who was truly a son to me, went through a series of losses long before he died at the age of thirteen after a five-year battle with leukemia. The loss that hit him hardest came toward the end of the illness. A doctor chose to tell him that the nature of the radiation therapy he was receiving meant he would never be able to have children. Tamar was stunned, grieved, and distressed. As we drove home, he shared the doctor's words. Tears swelled in his eyes, seeming to beg the question, *Could this possibly be true?*

Losses like these grab and tear at our hearts in a way that leaves us chafed and raw.

Something is wrong with the world and we know it. If we were shaped by impersonal forces, accidents of a purely random evolutionary process, it might make sense to us that the world could not be other than it is. But there is something in us that cannot accept the world as it is. According to Christianity, the problem is that something is broken in every one of us, not an accessory or something peripheral, but something at the core of our humanity.

The Bible often uses the word *sin* to describe this essential problem, as well as other terms like *transgressions, offenses,* or the phrase *falling short.* The idea of sin seems old and tired, a concept fallen on hard times, relegated to the dusty halls of theological libraries. And the concept is unpopular for a lot of reasons. It is sometimes used by religious people as a club to beat others over the head. It is strongly associated with guilt and other highly unpopular ideas. And without the possibility of God and his grace, it only drives us more deeply into hopelessness about ourselves. Many Christians today prefer less weighted words, or describe sin simply as "missing the mark," based on a literal translation of the Greek word. We miss the mark by a little bit, don't quite hit the target. It doesn't sound particularly serious.

But I have to wonder why the word *sin* has endured, why thoughtful people have held on to it for so long.

Right out of residency, I saw a patient for the first time who had suffered from pain in multiple joints and had been diagnosed with a non-specific autoimmune disorder. She had been treated for seven years with strong steroids. Since I could not find an appropriate work-up in her chart, I referred her to a rheumatologist who correctly diagnosed her with rheumatoid arthritis. Because she had originally been given the wrong diagnosis, two things had happened. First, she had received the wrong treatment, treatment with negative side effects and little benefit to her real condition. Second, she had *not* been receiving the right treatment, which might have improved her condition and limited the damage done by her disease.

We run the same risks when we don't understand what our real problem is. If we don't know what the problem is, we may not recognize the answer even if we find it. Whatever our understanding of the human dilemma, it is clear that the proper diagnosis of our condition is crucial to recognizing answers that might bring healing and allow us to move forward. Without an accurate diagnosis, we may choose to treat our condition with things that harm us or make us worse. Many things make us feel better for the moment, but often the things we desire most have the greatest power to destroy us.

The question must be asked: Does the concept of sin help us understand something about the human condition, something that makes a difference in diagnosis, something we may not be able to understand through any other approach? Is God in fact helping us by pointing out the reality of sin?

Looking Inside

Ernest Becker wrote that the most important and liberating question a human being can ask is the question of motive. Why do we do what we do? Any valid approach to the human condition must address this question of motivation for our action and choices. What makes us tick? What is the mainspring of human action? What drives us?

The biblical account of the fall of the human race pieces together parts of this puzzle in its description of Adam and Eve's choice to sin, providing insights that may be useful in helping us understand why we do what we do.

Now the serpent was more crafty than any of the wild animals the LORD God had made. He said to the woman, "Did God really say, 'You must not eat from any tree in the garden'?"

The woman said to the serpent, "We may eat fruit from the trees in the garden, but God did say, 'You must not eat fruit from the tree that is in the middle of the garden, and you must not touch it, or you will die.' "

"You will not certainly die," the serpent said to the woman. "For God knows that when you eat from it your eyes will be opened, and you will be like God, knowing good and evil."

When the woman saw that the fruit of the tree was good for food and pleasing to the eye, and also desirable for gaining wisdom, she took some and ate it. She also gave some to her husband, who was with her, and he ate it. Then the eyes of both of them were opened, and they realized they were naked; so they sewed fig leaves together and made coverings for themselves.

Then the man and his wife heard the sound of the LORD God as he was walking in the garden in the cool of the day, and they hid from the LORD God among the trees of the garden. But the LORD God called to the man, "Where are you?" (Genesis 3:1–9).

What were the driving forces behind Adam and Eve's choice to commit the first sin? First of all, human desire comes into play. The fruit was "pleasing to the eye." Desire is an essential part of our humanity. It animates us, it drives us. Christianity, unlike Buddhism and some other religious traditions, leaves no room for denial or repression of desire. The goal is not to minimize desire. In fact, desire is encouraged. Jesus tells us to ask, seek, knock, and find (Matthew 7:7–8). God draws us to himself by means of our deepest desires (Psalm 42:1–2; 63:1–3). In Christianity, the key is to pursue our desires in the right direction, the one set for us by God, toward the things that lead to life and have the potential to bring fulfillment.

Second, we witness Adam and Eve's specific desire to be something more than they were—an inability to accept their human limitations, a desire to be like God. Part of being human is the awareness of our mortality and the limitations of life. This awareness can either push us toward dependence on God or foster an inability to trust God to give us what we need, to be the kind of God we can live with. It can make us want to take things into our own hands.

Third, it is clear that Adam and Eve's sin had nothing to do with need or deprivation. The kind of wholeness and contentment described in Genesis was unlike anything any of us have ever known. In the perfect communion they had with their Creator, there was no reason for worry or anxiety. The choice they made was not a response to an external need or circumstance, but rather something within them.

This aspect of sin is described by Augustine in his *Confessions*. As a teenager, late one night he and some friends stole the pears from a neighbor's tree. He wrote,

> I was under no compulsion of need. . . . Yet I wanted to steal, and steal I did . . . we derived pleasure from the deed simply because it was forbidden. . . . Enable my heart to tell you now what it was seeking in this action which made me bad for no reason, in which there was no motive for my malice except malice. The malice was loathsome, and I loved it. I was in love with my own ruin, in love with decay . . . for I was depraved in soul.

The reason for the theft was not something external but something within Augustine.

What we see in the garden is a freedom to choose between right and wrong. We each have the capacity to choose between good and evil. But the reasons for the choices we make are at this level inexplicable. One prophet described the problem: "The heart is deceitful above all things and beyond cure. Who can understand it?" (Jeremiah 17:9).

This freedom is not only the grounds for personal responsibility, but without it our actions have no meaning. Adam and Eve had a real choice as to whether or not to sin, and so do we. There are always alternative courses of action to be evaluated and chosen. The social sciences have tried to eradicate this freedom through explanations of human behavior shaped by scientific determinism, arguing that we cannot do other than what we do. But this power of choice is necessary for any adequate understanding of the human condition. There is something within each person that exceeds the bounds of fate or determinism, reaching beyond the influences of emotions, upbringing, culture, and genetic predisposition.

Alexander Solzhenitsyn describes what he learned about human nature in the horrors of the Gulag, a Soviet labor camp where he was sent for criticizing Stalin. While a prisoner, as he recovered from surgery for cancer, he reflected on his life, repenting for what he did as a Red Army captain and comparing himself with the perpetrators of the Gulag. As I reviewed his life, I wanted to say, *You're not that bad. You're not like the evil oppressors in the Gulag.* But he was looking at his heart. Solzhenitsyn wrote, "It was granted to me to carry away from my prison years on my bent back, which nearly broke beneath its load, this essential experience: how a human being becomes evil and how good. In the intoxication of youthful successes, I had felt myself to be infallible, and I was therefore cruel. In the surfeit of power I was a murderer and an oppressor. In my most evil moments, I was convinced that I was doing good and I was well supplied with systematic arguments. It was only when I lay there on rotting prison straw that I sensed within myself the first stirrings of good. Gradually it was disclosed to me that the line separating good and evil passes not through states, nor between classes, nor between political parties either, but right through every human heart, and through all human hearts."

Finally, there is an element of spiritual influences and conflict—the craftiness of the serpent and human vulnerability to deception. The serpent's cunning and deceit was the first movement in an all-out battle for the allegiance and spiritual well-being of the human race. And in this battle, truth matters. Our presuppositions—what we do and do not know—play a role in our choices. It is interesting to see how the apostle Peter continually connects sin with ignorance while pointing to the transforming nature of the truth.

> Therefore, with *minds* that are alert and fully sober, set your hope
> on the grace to be brought to you when Jesus Christ is revealed at his
> coming. As obedient children, do not conform to the evil desires you
> had when you lived in *ignorance*. But just as he who called you is holy,

so be holy in all you do; for it is written: "Be holy, because I am holy" (1 Peter 1:13–16).

The wholeness that characterized life in the garden was interrupted by the choice to disobey the one thing God had asked. It was a choice based on a lack of trust, motivated by an inability to accept our limits, placing ourselves at the center; a choice to replace God with someone more compliant with our wishes. As a result, something was broken in us and this broken condition has led to dysfunction at every conceivable level of human existence.

When God Is Replaced

The question of God, whether or not he exists and what he is like, is the ultimate issue for humanity. As A. W. Tozer put it, "What comes into our minds when we think about God is the most important thing about us." Even if we claim *not* to believe in God, that belief impacts us profoundly. When we deny the existence of God, we reject the possibility of moral absolutes, ultimate meaning, and life beyond death.

What happens when we tear God from his rightful place? The inevitable result is the damaging of our lives—spiritually, physically, morally, intellectually, emotionally, and relationally.

Spiritually, the result is *idolatry*. Blaise Pascal describes the problem as a vacuum in the human soul:

> What else does this craving, and this helplessness, proclaim but that there was once in man a true happiness, of which all that now remains is the empty print and trace?
> This he tries in vain to fill with everything around him, seeking in things that are not there the help he cannot find in those that are, though none can help, since this infinite abyss can be filled only with an infinite and immutable object; in other words by God himself.

We cannot tolerate this God-shaped hole inside. We endeavor to fill it with whatever we can find that might ease our pain and anxiety. Our idols are the things we love more than God, prefer over God, the things we turn to for help, the things that shape our identity outside of God. As people created by God, in the image of God, for relationship with God, and to reflect the glory of God, the only sufficient ground for our identity is in this relationship. In our fallen state of anxiety, vulnerability, and helplessness, we begin to look for something to fill the void. We participate in all sorts of God-replacing activity, forming addictive attachments and trying to transcend frustration, anxiety, and a sense of futility by feeding our desires.

We are created in such a way that we will worship someone or something. In his commentary on Romans, Paul Achtemeier writes, "The root of our problem is the human propensity to put non-gods in the place of God. Such idolatry clearly means the rejection of the Creator for a deity more pliable to our wishes. Basically, idolatry means *not trusting God to be the kind of God we can live with.*" The tragedy of such idolatry, and the problem at the heart of the human dilemma, is that we have exchanged the loving, life-giving lordship of the God who created us for the lordship of something less than God—something that is not only incapable of meeting our needs but which will ultimately destroy us.

Physically, our substitutions for God express themselves as *addiction.* The emptiness, the restlessness inside will drive us to fill that intolerable hole in our souls with something. Augustine explained that a soul made by God for himself cannot be filled up by anything less than God himself. C. S. Lewis wrote, "A car is made to run on gasoline, and it would not run properly on anything else. Now, God designed the human machine to run on himself. He himself is the fuel our spirits were designed to burn, or the food our spirits were designed to feed on. There is no other."

Like nature, the human spirit abhors a vacuum. When we repress our longing for God we end up forming attachments with alternative deities. All of our appetites and desires become dysfunctional. We are driven by what French philosopher Jacques Ellul terms "consumer persistence." There must be something out there that will fulfill me, some thing, some experience, that next purchase, that one thing that will erase the nagging sense of emptiness.

The chaos of our inner life can be temporarily relieved by the sedating, numbing effects of all sorts of addictive attachments—food, alcohol, entertainment, television, materialism, accomplishment, busyness, drugs, and the misuse of our sexuality, to name a few. But because these things cannot satisfy our souls as God does, they tend to be abused rather than enjoyed. They often become the focal point of an escalating cycle of dependence that eventually consumes us. Gerald May, MD, in *Addiction and Grace*, plainly states that addiction is a form of idolatry that impacts every person.

> I am not being flippant when I say that all of us suffer from addiction. Nor am I reducing the meaning of addiction. I mean in all truth that the psychological, neurological, and spiritual dynamics of full-fledged addiction are actively at work within every human being. . . . Addiction also makes idolaters of us all, because it forces us to worship these objects of attachment, thereby preventing us from truly, freely loving God and one another. Addiction breeds willfulness within us, yet again paradoxically, it erodes our free will and eats away our dignity.

When God is taken out of the picture, *morally* we move toward *relativism*. Without God there are no moral absolutes, no truths that are always true for everyone. Without God, we become the measure of reality—what we think, what we feel, what we "believe." Things are "true" to the extent that they seem "good" to us, make us happy, and contribute to our well-being.

Intellectually, life without God leads to a *loss of meaning*. If we are a chance configuration of matter, an accident of some impersonal evolutionary process, then there is no reason to believe that life has any ultimate meaning.

The kind of humanism most typically encountered today, with its emphasis on human experience and reason, and skepticism about all other sources of truth, often focuses on the possibility of purpose and meaning in the specialness of human beings and their unique abilities—language, creativity, reason, culture, technology, values, and the ability to love. No doubt, these capacities are clues to the dignity and specialness of humankind. Many people who reject the possibility of God find a sense of meaning in the choice to help people by caring, feeding, and minimizing the suffering of these special beings. This makes some sense. God places great importance on our response to human need. Ironically, when humans are viewed by the secular mind as mere products of evolution, the result can also be a loss of this sense of human specialness. And the big rub is that even though humanism may provide some immediate sense of meaning for some people, there can be no ultimate meaning to human existence, even in this, without God.

Without God *emotionally*, we are faced with *boredom*. In a strictly material world without the possibility of the spiritual, we may easily develop an inability to see the miraculous, the joy-filled, the special in our day-to-day encounters. The sheer goodness of so much of life may be gutted by our loss of life's meaning and purpose. The absence of the spiritual and the miraculous can produce a familiarity that causes us to take life and people for granted. It seems to me that part of spiritual life is unlearning our familiarity and recovering the ability to see the world with a childlike sense of awe and wonder.

Without God *relationally*, we experience *isolation*. It is easy to think of the consequences of our own choices as affecting only ourselves. But sin has far-reaching consequences. The fall of man reminds us that a single act of sin reverberated through the universe, changing its very fabric.

What would happen if there was a completely good and perfectly competent being who was committed to our best interests and was always there to care for us? There would be no need for worry and anxiety. But when we remove such a being from the picture, we experience tremendous anxiety. This line of reasoning indicates to some that we tend to invent what we need most, and for others it seems an argument about human nature and the way we are made. Either way, left to ourselves and without God, there is no one left to take care of me but *me*. I quickly move toward self-absorption and behavior aimed at control—covering my nakedness and shame, hiding, blaming, arguing, fighting, even killing.

When Adam and Eve sinned, their relationship with God was damaged. They had shared the kind of friendship and intimacy that involved direct communication and daily walks together. All of that was ended by sin. And in destroying their relationship with God, they were faced with death. Sin not only leaves us beat up physically, spiritually, and emotionally, it kills us by separating us from God, who is life.

Their relationship with each other was also damaged. We read the first accounts of blame and strife and even murder between siblings.

Sin destroyed their relationship with self. Before sin, they worked and played in the garden—naked and without any sense of shame. When they sinned, they immediately felt the need to cover their nakedness and hide as they experienced the first pangs of guilt and shame.

Sin also destroyed their relationship with the created order. Before sin, when they planted corn, the corn grew, but after their sin, weeds grew up with the corn, and they had to work harder to have a good harvest.

Sin is a force that is destructive of relationship. Sin has cosmic consequences, so that "we are all prisoners of sin" (Galatians 3:22 NLT), causing all of creation to long to be "liberated from its bondage to decay" (Romans 8:21).

A few years ago, one of my partners asked if I would be willing to take over the care of a patient that she was finding particularly difficult. The patient was continually angry and threatening, but my partner felt that I might be able to work with her. The situation was worse than I expected. The first time I walked into the exam room, this woman was sitting on the exam table visibly angry, and she began to complain bitterly about the problems she had with other doctors. She might as well have had the word *lawsuit* tattooed on her forehead. I took a brief history and asked her to come back every other week until we sorted out all of her concerns. Over the first couple of months we established some trust and identified her medical problems. One of the main problems she needed to face was her alcoholism. I recommended that she start attending AA every day. She was very lonely and isolated—divorced, alienated from her two adult children, and with no real friends. I explained that in the process of recovery she would need emotional and spiritual support and recommended that she also start attending a church.

Soon after that she disappeared for about six weeks. What I experienced when she returned for an appointment was one of the most stunning events of my professional life. I walked into the exam room and almost didn't recognize her. She had a new haircut; there was a new softness in her face and a sense of peace that transformed her appearance. She spoke with a gentleness I had never heard in her speech before. We sat and talked. She said she was doing much better. She explained that she had gone to the Calvary Chapel near her apartment. She said, "I did this thing they call 'giving your life to Jesus.' " She described the sense of forgiveness that had come over her, freedom from guilt, hope for the future, hope for her relationships with her kids, the beginning of the end of loneliness. God had moved back in and everything was different. She had all of the same problems and challenges, but a new relationship, a source of strength, a reason for hope. She has been sober for two years, and is one of the most delightful people I know.

Ultimately, the displacement of God leads to *futility*, especially in the face of death. Leo Tolstoy, at the age of fifty-one, after writing *War and Peace* and *Anna Karenina*, came to believe he had accomplished nothing in his life. As he struggled with this anxiety about the meaning of his life, he lamented in his book *Confession*: "What will come of what I do today and tomorrow? What will come of my entire life? Expressed differently, the question may be: Why should I live? Why should I wish for anything or do anything? Or to put it still another way: Is there any meaning in my life that will not be destroyed by my inevitably approaching death?" Psychologist William James describes death as "the worm at the core" of all the things in life that might make us happy.

Think of the effects of a single sin on the part of Adam and Eve as they made the choice to violate the one command God had given them

(Genesis 3). Everything changed. Like a contagion, sin inserted itself in the human spirit and invaded creation, producing a society characterized by wickedness and a way of life so regrettable to God that it ultimately led to judgment and global destruction. "Every inclination of the thoughts of the human heart was only evil all the time" (Genesis 6:5). The effects of sin are more far-reaching than we realize.

There is a reason God hates sin. There is a reason for his costly response to human need. There is a reason for his efforts to point us in the right direction. Sin makes life ugly. It destroys relationships and it destroys lives. It is the root cause of all that is disturbing, revolting, and unacceptable in the world.

We live in a world of desperate need—spiritual lostness and confusion, death, hunger, poverty, ignorance, disease, a lack of compassion, isolation, loneliness, emotional pain, and loss of meaning to life. And we have underestimated God's hatred of evil. Things like starvation, disease, and the trafficking of children are not merely variations on normal that God tolerates, but forms of evil that God loathes and which he will ultimately destroy. These things must be opposed and fought by every loving heart.

Speaking hypothetically, if we were asked to write a story that would account for the condition of the human race today, we would end up with something remarkably similar to the biblical description of the fall. It seems to me that word for word this account explains more about the human condition than anything else I have ever read.

Getting Us Back on Course

To summarize, sin is any departure from life as God intends it. It is misusing our freedom, producing the kinds of consequences we often describe as evil. It is plunging over the guardrail God has erected to keep us from falling into great peril physically, emotionally, and spiritually. It is the root cause of all death—physical and spiritual. And sin lies at the core of many of our deepest problems—fear, loneliness, isolation, guilt, shame, and lack of purpose and meaning.

As people created by God, in the image of God, for relationship with God, we need his help. We need the instruction manual written by the one who designed us. The law and God's instruction to us in Scripture—the wisdom literature, including the didactic Psalms, Proverbs, Ecclesiastes, James, the parables and teachings of Jesus, and the ethical teaching of the epistles—are God's help in keeping us from destroying ourselves and each other.

Another of the most important questions we can ask ourselves is simply, *Is it the wise thing to do?* Just because we *can* do a thing does not mean we *should* do it. So much of life's suffering could be eliminated by simply asking this question and weighing our choices and actions against a reliable and valid standard of wisdom or morality, providing the protective effect of biblical wisdom. I recently read a brief story about Albert Einstein that struck right at the heart of wisdom's meaning. When the bombing of Hiroshima occurred, Einstein was working. An American general rushed in to inform him of events, telex in hand. Einstein held his head in his hands in silence for a long period and finally said: "The old Chinese were right: You cannot do whatever you want."

I have often heard it said in reference to human failure, that we are "only human." But this sets our sights much too low. To be human is to live out what it means to be created in the image of God, to reflect something of his glory. And to sin is to be less than human, less than what we were created to be. We are what we are, but God intends for us to be something more, something new, people who are no longer broken.

The law functions graciously to protect our relationships with God, others, self, and creation. But it also helps us understand ourselves by shedding light on our inability to do what it asks so much of the time. It exposes our brokenness and sinfulness. Ultimately this sense of need reveals our need for Jesus. In fact, Paul says that the law was given to lead us to Christ (Galatians 3:24). From a Christian point of view, the ultimate purpose of the law is not to save us but to point us to our need of grace. Paul wrote that "a person is not justified by the works of the law, but by faith in Jesus Christ. So we, too, have put our faith in Christ Jesus that we may be justified by faith in

Christ and not by the works of the law, because by the works of the law no one will be justified" (Galatians 2:16). Luther summarized the matter well: "The principal point . . . of the law . . . is to make people not better but worse; that is to say it shows them their sin, so that by their knowledge of sin they might be humbled, terrified, bruised and broken, and by this means might be driven to seek grace and so come to Christ."

An important part of moving toward wholeness is understanding the problem of sin. There is no kindness in minimizing sin or its effects, because in doing so we fail to warn others of its destructive potential. Dietrich Bonhoeffer wrote in *Life Together*, "Nothing can be more cruel than the tenderness that consigns another to his sin. Nothing can be more compassionate than the severe rebuke that calls a brother back from the path of sin." A part of loving people well is finding the courage to lovingly confront harmful behavior. Henri Nouwen wrote,

> Perhaps the main task of the minister is to prevent people from suffering for the wrong reasons. Many people suffer because of the false supposition on which they have based their lives. . . . Therefore ministry is a very confronting service. It does not allow people to live with illusions of immortality and wholeness. It keeps reminding others that they are mortal and broken, but also that with the recognition of this condition, liberation starts.

The Quiet Intersection

What we are trying to do throughout this book is discover some insight into the human dilemma at the intersection of theology and science; but put simply, on the subject of sin it is a very quiet intersection. What one generally finds in modern psychology and psychiatry is the rejection of ideas like sin, morality, virtue, and responsibility. These concepts are viewed as relics of outdated religious traditions. But if we listen carefully, we do hear a few voices breaking through the silence.

In the 1960s, O. Hobart Mowrer, writing as a psychologist to psychologists, explained that the reality of sin may be foundational to a sense of self:

> For several decades we psychologists looked upon the whole matter of sin and moral accountability as a great incubus and acclaimed our liberation from it as epoch-making. But at length we have discovered that to be "free" in this sense, i.e., to have the excuse of being "sick" rather than *sinful,* is to court the danger of becoming *lost.* . . . In becoming amoral, ethically neutral, and "free," we have cut the very roots of being; lost our deepest sense of selfhood and identity; and, with neurotics themselves, find ourselves asking: "Who *am* I? What is my *destiny?* What does living (existence) *mean?*"

In other words, when we eliminate concepts like *guilt* and *sin,* we may define away so much of what it is to be human that our identity is completely lost. Physician, psychologist, and philosopher William James made the same argument when he wrote: "Healthy-mindedness is inadequate as a philosophical doctrine" to the extent that it denies the "evil facts" that are "a genuine portion of reality" and that these facts may provide the "best key to life's significance, and possibly the only openers of our eyes to the deepest levels of truth." Without grasping and acknowledging all aspects of human experience, we may never understand what it is to be human.

And with this loss of identity and meaning comes the sensation that the writer of Ecclesiastes describes with the Hebrew word *hebel,* literally "vapor" or "smoke," that sense of meaninglessness (Ecclesiastes 1:2), emptiness, unsubstantiality, and the fragility of life. Again, nothing can be found to fill up that God-shaped hole inside of us. We use whatever we can to this end, but our successes are empty, our marriages strained by our neediness, and our children stressed by the extent to which we base our own happiness on their success. Money and materialism prove incongruent with our deepest needs, and even churches become characterized by a consumer mentality among people searching for the church that will do things the way they want, the way they need them done. Nothing can be found to fill the emptiness.

We long for something more. This longing is perhaps best explained by what the writer of Ecclesiastes describes as God having "set eternity in the human heart" (Ecclesiastes 3:11)—a thirst for something lasting, a longing for some meaning that will transcend death, an insistence that there is more to this life than living briefly, working, sweating, loving, and dying.

Mowrer also argued that neurosis is often the result of immoral behavior, and that the ability to acknowledge sin and guilt is a psychologically necessary step in the process of moving beyond remorse and shame:

> Recovery (constructive change, redemption) is most assuredly attained, not by helping a person reject and rise above his sins, but by helping him *accept them*. This is the paradox which we have not at all understood and which is the very crux of the problem. Just so long as a person lives under the shadow of real, unacknowledged, and unexpiated guilt, he *cannot* (if he has any character at all) "accept himself," and all *our* efforts to reassure and accept him will avail nothing. He will continue to hate himself and to suffer the inevitable consequences of self-hatred. But the moment he (with or without "assistance") begins to accept his guilt and sinfulness, the possibility of radical reformation opens up; and with this, the individual may legitimately, though not without pain and effort, pass from deep, pervasive self-rejection and self-torture to a new freedom of self-respect and peace.

In 1975, Donald Campbell echoed some of the same ideas. He addressed the American Psychological Association as its newly elected president in a speech he described as a "broad brush speculative talk dealing with human nature."

> Present-day psychology and psychiatry in all their major forms are more hostile to the inhibitory messages of traditional religious moralizing than is scientifically justified . . . in the areas of disagreement (as to how people should live their lives, child rearing, sex, duty, guilt, sin, self-indulgence, etc.), we are unable to experiment or in other ways to put well-developed theories to rigorous test. On these issues, psychology and psychiatry cannot yet claim to be truly scientific and thus have special reasons for modesty and caution in undermining traditional

belief systems. . . . The religions of all ancient urban civilizations . . . taught that many aspects of human nature need to be curbed if optimal social coordination is to be achieved; for example, selfishness, pride, greed, dishonesty, covetousness, cowardice, lust, wrath. Psychology and psychiatry, on the other hand, not only describe man as selfishly motivated, but implicitly or explicitly teach that he ought to be so. They tend to see repression and inhibition of the individual impulse as undesirable, and see all guilt as a dysfunctional neurotic blight created by cruel child rearing and a needlessly repressive society. They further recommend that we accept our biological and psychological impulses as good and seek pleasure rather than enchain ourselves with duty.

I cannot help but wonder why these two men, so fully given to scientific endeavor, were able to recognize the need to look beyond the confines of science for the answer to the human problem. Two simple statements, one from each writer, provide the answer.

Campbell described religious morals as "recipes for living . . . that have been evolved, tested, and winnowed through hundreds of generations of human social history." He concludes that "on purely scientific grounds, these recipes for living might be regarded as better tested than the best of psychology's and psychiatry's speculations on how lives should be lived."

Similarly, Mowrer wrote that "since this matter of man's total adjustment and psychosocial survival does not quickly yield up its innermost secrets to conventional types of scientific inquiry, I believe it will do no harm for us at the same time to be thinking about some frankly ideological matters."

They share a common presupposition, a sense that science cannot provide ultimate answers about the meaning of human existence. For those who believe we were designed by a personal God rather than impersonal forces, this makes good sense. Science alone can't provide the answers to the issues that matter most to us. Both men, though committed to the relevance of scientific insight into human behavior, share an intellectual humility that freed them to look beyond science. This insight is described by the writer of Ecclesiastes:

When I applied my mind to know wisdom and to observe the labor that is done on earth—people getting no sleep day or night—then I saw all that God has done. No one can comprehend what goes on under the sun. Despite all their efforts to search it out, no one can discover its meaning. Even if the wise claim they know, they cannot really comprehend it. (Ecclesiastes 8:16–17)

What Science Can and Cannot Do

At one level, science is a process of learning how much we do not know. With each new discovery dozens if not hundreds of new questions arise. Science has tremendous value and concrete benefits. But among its limits is that it cannot explain ultimate reality and meaning. In fact, to the extent that science views nature as merely physical, it denies ultimate meaning; therefore, making a religion out of it is pointless. Separating science and wisdom, the physical and the spiritual, is a serious error from the standpoint of both science and spirituality. And when Mowrer and Campbell realized this, they hit pay dirt in their quest for a sense of meaning and identity.

There are other ways we may ask too much of science. Another false hope based on human optimism and scientific advancement is the myth of progress rooted in a belief in unlimited human potential to improve our own condition. This road is futile because it offers no answer to the problem of evil. It provides no meaningful explanation for or remedy to the problems in human nature that have produced slavery, drug trafficking, war, genocide, child abuse, and other evidences of what goes on inside a person.

On the other side of the coin is the danger of the pessimism that grows out of determinism, the belief that things are as they are and cannot be otherwise. Determinism, whether it is rooted in a scientific model or a theological dogma, has the effect of robbing us of hope and any basis for believing that things can change. The Christian view is simply that there is a God who is competent and powerful and willing and able to intervene in the natural course of events. Faith in Jesus therefore engages the individual and group in rejecting the status quo, refusing to accept the world as it is in its fallenness. Because God is, our choices matter. Things can change. There is reason for hope.

The way Christians rebel against the status quo is (a) through obedience to God's way of doing things by which we facilitate his kingdom righteousness and justice, (b) through prayer, by which we invite his power and the coming of his kingdom, and (c) through the proclamation of the gospel, which is good news about the goodness, competence, and willingness of God to take broken, sinful people and give them a new start and a new life. God is at work in us and through us to make everything new—to restore our relationships with him, self, others, and creation.

The first step on the road toward the life God intends is realizing that we have a problem so big that we cannot save ourselves. As Paul explains:

> At one time we too were foolish, disobedient, deceived and enslaved by all kinds of passions and pleasures. We lived in malice and envy, being hated and hating one another. But when the kindness and love of God our Savior appeared, he saved us, not because of righteous things we had done, but because of his mercy. He saved us through the washing of rebirth and renewal by the Holy Spirit, whom he poured out on us generously through Jesus Christ our Savior, so that, having been justified by his grace, we might become heirs having the hope of eternal life. (Titus 3:3–7)

Our purpose in this book is to discover and evaluate some aspects of the best possible life and to consider the ways in which the literature and discoveries of the sciences demonstrate the kindness of the law and God's instructions to us. But what we discover in the process is that the way to purpose, meaning, and wholeness begins not in changing our behavior, but in returning to the God that made us, establishing our life and hope and identity in him and in his love expressed in the gospel. God's grace makes us a new creation, and biblical wisdom offers us direction in working out that newness in all of our relationships.

two

WHY FORGIVE?

*And when you stand praying, if you hold anything against
anyone, forgive them, so that your Father in heaven
may forgive you your sins.*
(MARK 11:25)

Forgiven

Forgiveness has nothing to do with forgetting or ignoring the wrong others do. It's about seeing our own failures in a way that leads us to show grace when others fail us. The better we understand our real condition, the more fully we grasp our own need of grace and forgiveness. Being honest about who we are and what we are invites grace, and grace leads to humility, because grace makes no sense. I can't earn it or deserve it. And if I don't earn it or deserve it, who am I to withhold it from someone else?

We cannot understand God's instructions to forgive others without understanding something about what he is like, his own forgiving nature. The foundation for human forgiveness is the character of God. Psalm 103:8–14 tells us:

The LORD is compassionate and gracious,
slow to anger, abounding in love.
He will not always accuse,
nor will he harbor his anger forever;
he does not treat us as our sins deserve
or repay us according to our iniquities.
For as high as the heavens are above the earth,
so great is his love for those who fear him;
as far as the east is from the west,
so far has he removed our transgressions from us.
As a father has compassion on his children,
so the LORD has compassion on those who fear him;
for he knows how we are formed,
he remembers that we are dust.

Because he is gracious he "forgives all your sins and heals all your diseases," he "redeems your life from the pit and crowns you with love and compassion" (Psalm 103:1–4).

Nehemiah describes God as "a forgiving God, gracious and compassionate, slow to anger and abounding in love," not deserting even the arrogant, stiff-necked, and rebellious people who blasphemed against God and worshiped a golden calf, claiming that the idol had rescued them from Egypt. God did not abandon them in the wilderness. He forgave them (Nehemiah 9:17–19).

King David, described as a man after God's own heart, needed God's forgiveness as much as any of us. At a point in his life when things were going well, he committed adultery and then had the woman's husband killed in battle. David's confession of this sin is rooted in the same confidence about God's character and his willingness to forgive.

Have mercy on me, O God,
according to your unfailing love;
according to your great compassion
blot out my transgressions.
Wash away all my iniquity
and cleanse me from my sin.

> For I know my transgressions,
> and my sin is always before me.
> Against you, you only, have I sinned
> and done what is evil in your sight;
> so you are right in your verdict
> and justified when you judge. (Psalm 51:1–4)

When David confesses to God, "against you, you only, have I sinned," he acknowledges that all sin is ultimately against God, an affront to his holiness. But David also grasped God's mercy and his willingness to forgive. He was honest about his own sin and aware of the need for grace.

One has to ask how God is able to forgive, to look beyond our sin and restore a relationship with us. The problem is that a holy, righteous God cannot simply overlook sin and turn a blind eye to evil. Moshe Halbertal and Avishai Margalit raise this question in their book *Idolatry*. In the book of Ezekiel, God likens idolatry to the relationship between a husband and wife. Halbertal and Margalit ask, "If God and Israel are husband and wife and the wife committed adultery, then reconciliation seems impossible . . . how is it possible according to biblical law, for an adulterous wife to return to her husband?" Job asked the same question: "How can mere mortals prove their innocence before God?" (Job 9:2).

This question is the context for much of the New Testament. God cannot simply overlook sin and remain righteous and just. *Let's just pretend that never happened.* Sin means we are not right; we are "unrighteous." What we need is to be made right. Weighing and measuring the good in our lives and hoping that it somehow outweighs the bad cannot solve the problem. Sin leads to death and separation from God, and no amount of "good" can undo the problem and reverse sin's impact on our condition. We are spiritually dead and separated from God and have nothing to bring to the table.

Paul wrote in Romans 3 what Leon Morris describes as "possibly the most important single paragraph ever written."

But now apart from the law the righteousness of God has been made known, to which the Law and the Prophets testify. This righteousness is given through faith in Jesus Christ to all who believe. There is no difference between Jew and Gentile, for all have sinned and fall short of the glory of God, and all are justified freely by his grace through the redemption that came by Christ Jesus. God presented Christ as a sacrifice of atonement, through the shedding of his blood—to be received by faith. He did this to demonstrate his righteousness, because in his forbearance he had left the sins committed beforehand unpunished—he did it to demonstrate his righteousness at the present time, so as to be just and the one who justifies those who have faith in Jesus. (Romans 3:21–26)

This is God's response to the human condition. He does not leave us stuck in the dilemma caused by sin. He provides a way to make sinners righteous while maintaining his own righteousness and justice. He does this while we are powerless, absolutely helpless, and unable to rescue ourselves. "You see, at just the right time, when we were still powerless, Christ died for the ungodly. Very rarely will anyone die for a righteous person, though for a good person someone might possibly dare to die. But God demonstrates his own love for us in this: While we were still sinners, Christ died for us" (Romans 5:6–8).

For me, Romans 5:8 is the most radical statement in all of Scripture. Before we cared about God, before we gave him a thought, or gave a rip about what he thought, while we were still enemies, God chose to demonstrate his love. We did nothing to deserve it, nothing to earn it. He loved us before we did anything, and it had nothing to do with anything good or winsome or compelling on our part.

John Stott describes *justification* as the means by which a righteous God righteously "righteouses" unrighteous people. On the cross, God was giving himself to us, embracing the horror of sin-bearing death, and doing it all for his undeserving enemies. The cross was no accident. It embodies the costly choice made by God to send his Son to deal with the problem of sin, the willingness of the Son to empty himself of all that was not essential to his divinity and to die in our place. Because of the cross we can live as forgiven people, a new creation.

One way to think of what happens at the cross is described by theologians as *imputation*. Paul put it like this: "God made him (Jesus) who had no sin to be sin for us, so that in him we might become the righteousness of God" (2 Corinthians 5:21). In other words, Jesus, the only righteous one, the only one who did everything right, is made not right so that the ones who were not right might be made right. The Son, because of our sin, was treated like an enemy so that we who were the enemies might be treated like sons and daughters. The one who had the approval of God took on our condemnation so that we, the condemned ones, might receive God's approval. God treated Jesus like he lived our lives so that he might treat us like we had lived Jesus' life.

This is the gospel, what Paul described as the best and most important news we will ever hear—that God would place our sin and guilt upon Jesus so that he might place his righteousness upon us. And this unbelievable gift is ours by faith.

The gospel means that we have nothing to fear from anyone, that only God's opinion of us matters. Because of what Jesus has done, he has called us righteous. The "very good" pronounced by God at creation has been restored, and we can actually stand before the God of the universe and hear him say, "I commend you, I accept you, I am pleased with you."

C. S. Lewis, in one of his essays, "The Weight of Glory," described the day when we will stand before the holy, righteous God:

> The promise of glory is the promise, almost incredible and only possible by the work of Christ, that some of us, that any of us who really chooses, shall actually survive that examination, shall find approval, shall please God. To please God . . . to be a real ingredient in the divine happiness . . . to be loved by God, not merely pitied, but delighted in as an artist delights in his work or a father in a son—it seems impossible, a weight or burden of glory which our thoughts can hardly sustain. But so it is.

When God's love demonstrated by Jesus becomes the deepest awareness of yourself—that you are justified, accepted, and approved, and that you are a child of God—when this truth falls into you, displacing all other definitions of yourself, then your identity is in Jesus and you are set free. You are not who you were. You are a new creation (2 Corinthians 5:17). You are "the righteousness of God" in Christ (2 Corinthians 5:21).

The recognition of this truth has been tough for me, my capacity for trust badly frayed by my early experiences of life. As a young adult I carried around a sense of invincibility characteristic of youth, which in part expressed itself in me as a belief that I had escaped the trauma of childhood unscathed and that I was just fine.

When I came to Fuller Seminary as a student in my early twenties, I found the first time and space in my life in which I felt perfectly safe. I found men and women, including faculty, that extended love, respect, and grace—Colin and Olive Brown, Jim Bradley, Ruth Fuglie Netting Vuong, and others. The irony of my experience of safety was that there in a sanctuary of rest and peace, the bottom fell out as I came to grips with my wretchedness and brokenness, the damage done to my soul by my own sin and the sins of others. Not only was I able to see it, but I was able to speak of the guarded secrets of my past for the first time, secrets so dark and disturbing to me that I thought I might die of fear and pain if I were to speak of them. I tapped into an insatiable need and longing for grace infinitely deeper than what I had known before. And there tremendous healing began.

For a long time this made little sense to me. Why in this safe place were my eyes open to the truth about my condition? That's the paradox of grace. It is that crazy, intangible thing that we cannot earn, deserve, or buy. It's a gift—the one thing we need more than anything else, but something we cannot obtain on our own. And when we find it and really understand it, when it falls into us, displacing fear and every other way of defining ourselves, it sets us free. And because we can't earn it, because it's not about us or our virtue or our ability to get things right, because it is about what Jesus has done, we no longer have to hide. There is no need to pretend, or care about what anyone else thinks. We can let go of our need to be right, to prove ourselves, to come out on top. We are truly free. William James described this liberating experience:

> To give up one's pretensions is as blessed a relief as to get them gratified, and where disappointment is incessant and the struggle unending, that is what men will always do. The history of evangelical theology, with its conviction of sin, its self-despair, and its abandonment of salvation by works, is the deepest of possible examples.

The relief found in coming to terms with my sin and brokenness was overwhelming. The death of pretense is at once excruciating and relieving, the tearing from our hearts our most reliable and trusted defenses—exchanging self-deception for transparency, pride for peace and rest, the need to prove oneself for the embrace of God.

> My heart is not proud, LORD,
> my eyes are not haughty;
> I do not concern myself with great matters
> or things too wonderful for me.
>
> But I have calmed and quieted myself;
> like a weaned child with its mother,
> like a weaned child is my soul within me. (Psalm 131:1–2)

A Universal Need

Several years ago, I began working with a new patient whose primary need was not physical. Susan was twenty-one. As she sat down in my office, she began to cry and continued for about ten minutes. When she was finally able to speak, she shared with me that she had had an abortion a few weeks earlier, and that she felt a deep sense of both regret and guilt. The emotional pain seemed to be getting worse with time.

As a child, she had attended church on holidays, but had not attended church at all for years. She felt isolated from her boyfriend, who had rejected her when she became pregnant, and from her parents, since she felt that she could not tell them what had happened. And she believed that God must be angry with her, and even wondered if he would allow her to have any children in the future after what she had done. Her face had the drawn expression of someone who had been beaten up emotionally.

What she needed most was forgiveness. She needed to know that God could and would forgive her, that her parents might see her once again as their beloved daughter and continue to love and care for her, and that the rest of her life would not be destroyed by the choices she had made. Thankfully, Susan found the forgiveness she needed in a relationship with Jesus, through the love and care of her parents, and through a gracious counselor. I encouraged her to stop trying to save herself by inflicting pain, guilt, and self-contempt and instead look to Jesus and embrace his forgiveness and grace. As she began to read the Bible, she learned that God's grace was greater than any sin in her life and that every moment in the presence of God is an opportunity to have our eternal destinies shaped by what happens from this moment forward rather than by anything in our past.

We all come to these places of need. Even the atheist, the moral relativist, the skeptic, and the anti-religious experience guilt and regret. I have never talked with anyone who was able to tell me that they never experienced these feelings. Even people who learn to ignore the deep rumblings within find them bubbling up to the surface in times of crisis and loss. Like the rest of us, they need forgiveness—a sense that they're forgiven by God and others—as well as the ability to forgive themselves. And Jesus has opened up the only path to forgiveness by what he has done for us.

Even people who follow Jesus may continue to experience feelings of persistent guilt, shame, inferiority, and inadequacy. Part of my life has been marked by a struggle for self-forgiveness and a resistance to grace. In particular, I have trouble forgiving the pain I caused other people years ago through my dishonesty. While growing up with an angry, alcoholic father, I found it easier and less painful to tell him what he wanted to hear than to tell him the truth. But my relationship with my father was only the context. The choice to lie was still mine, and the habit I developed carried over into other relationships. Treasured friendships were damaged or destroyed by my dishonesty.

Sometimes Christians get it backwards. We work hard at obedience to find the grace we need. But the Christian life is a response to grace not a way to earn grace. Grace leads to obedience. Pastor and author Tim Keller says, "Religion operates on the principle 'I obey—therefore I am accepted by God.' But the operating principle of the gospel is 'I am accepted by God through what Christ has done—therefore I obey.' "

For years I could not forgive myself for the hurt I had caused. I had many wounds, atrocious hurts inflicted by others that had healed long ago—but this one would not heal. I realized that the unhealed wound had to do with my own self-condemnation. The wounds involving the failures of others had been easier to heal. I could forgive them. I just could not forgive myself. I must have assumed things about God that were not true. I had to wonder, if we cannot forgive ourselves, have we really trusted Jesus, trusted in God's forgiveness of us? And if we don't trust in God's forgiveness, how can we believe him when he says he wants an intimate relationship with us?

Living with inappropriate guilt causes us to be afraid of God. It creates a sense of distance in our relationship with him. As I began to look to Jesus, focusing on the reality of God's forgiveness and applying it to the wound, it began to heal. But I am still aware of the resistance of my own soul to God's grace at times.

Forgiving

Paul connects the way God forgives us with the way we respond to the people who hurt us. "Be kind and compassionate to one another, forgiving each other, just as in Christ God forgave you" (Ephesians 4:32). "Bear with each other and forgive one another if any of you has a grievance against someone. Forgive as the Lord forgave you" (Colossians 3:13).

Part of living lives defined by the gospel is demonstrating to others the grace shown to us by God.

But forgiveness is not easy. C. S. Lewis wrote, "Everyone says forgiveness is a lovely idea, until they have something to forgive." Without forgiveness we are left to the law of the playground—he hit me harder than I hit him so I have to hit him harder—and this law of the playground is the law of groups and nations. We are left to an ever-escalating cycle of injury and hatred. Evil is like a piece of counterfeit currency passed around from person to person, because no one is willing to absorb the loss. Only Jesus, who never injured another, can step in and say, "I will take the loss. I will take upon myself all of the evil of humanity with all of its effects. I will bear it all and absorb the injury."

Forgiveness has at least two parts—the initial decision and the follow through. When we choose to forgive we choose to release the other person from the consequences of the way their actions affected us, letting go of our hurt, anger, and desire for revenge. We choose to see the offender apart from our pain and anger. But forgiveness is not denial of our pain and loss, nor is it pretending that it never happened. It is a choice that requires tremendous courage and honesty.

And forgiveness requires follow through on the initial decision because there may be times we want to take up the offense again. Forgiveness means choosing to live out each moment and each encounter in the grace of our initial choice. We persist in our refusal to let the relationship be defined by our pain.

Forgiveness is not reconciliation. I can forgive unilaterally, even in the absence of sorrow or repentance on the part of the offender. I can choose to forgive and let go of my pain and anger. But reconciliation requires two people facing honestly the nature of the offense—repentance from the offender, and forgiveness from the offended. When appropriate, there should also be amends or restitution, and hopefully, the rebuilding of trust. Personal forgiveness does not necessarily release the one forgiven from the legal and civil consequences of their sin.

By the time I was eighteen my relationship with my father was over.

The anger and verbal abuse and physical violence triggered by his problem with alcohol had wounded me so deeply that I was certain I would never have a meaningful relationship with him again. I was able to forgive, to let go of the pain of the past. But every time I attempted to address the past with him, I was met by a wall of anger and defensiveness. Our relationship was dead.

When I was in my late twenties, preparing to get married, I invited my father to come with me and talk with my counselor. I laid out my hurt and some of the painful facts of the past. Once again, he responded with anger and defensiveness. Wanting to spare me further pain, my counselor did not see any point in asking him back for a second visit, but I insisted and invited my father back anyway. At the second visit my father broke down and began to cry. He owned the past. In fact, he expanded the case against himself and asked for forgiveness.

His acknowledgment of reality caused a sensation of relief like a dislocated bone popping back into place. Something new was born that day. He has been sober now for decades and has grown into a loving father and grandfather. He loves Jesus passionately. No one who knows him today would ever guess the truth about the past if he didn't tell them, because he really is a different person. Twice a year we travel to visit him. Carole and our children love him, and my father and I have a good relationship. By God's grace, I love and respect my father.

Whether we are the offender or the offended party, Jesus places on us the responsibility to go directly to our brother or sister for the purpose of reconciliation. He asks us to leave our offering at the altar in order to be reconciled first with those who may have something against us before we offer our gift to God (Matthew 5:23–24). And when our brother or sister sins, Jesus asks us to first go and privately reprove that brother or sister with a view to winning them over before we do anything else (Matthew 18:15–17).

Some Christians think we should forgive only if the offender repents. Jesus does command us to forgive someone who repents, but he also asks us to forgive all the time, even in the absence of repentance (Matthew 6:14; 18:21–22; Mark 11:25; Luke 6:37; 11:4). Without their repentance, Jesus forgave the people who participated in killing him.

Deleo Moses Ocen is the director of Lifewater Partner Organization in Uganda. He tells his story, describing several aspects of the challenge of forgiveness. His family home was invaded and burned, and his mother viciously attacked with a spear and machete, causing internal bleeding, lacerations, and two broken arms. She was left for dead. His mother survived the attack. The attacker was tried and sent to prison. Deleo struggled to forgive the man, fasting and praying for a spirit of forgiveness. He writes:

> Four years later, word reached me that my mother's attacker had been prematurely released. I burned with anger. For weeks my mind was constantly seething and I felt that if I saw the man, I would kill him.
>
> One day as I was riding to town on my bicycle, I abruptly met my mother's attacker as I was going down a slope. Seeing him, I fainted and fell from my bicycle, creating teasing from onlookers. I turned around and went home. In my closet, I wept before God for my unforgiving heart. I asked Jesus to forgive me for harboring bitterness over my enemy.
>
> The message is that God forgives us, though we are thieves and murderers in our hearts, and in his grace requires us to forgive others in the same way. At first, I recoiled in anger, rejecting the message and refusing to release my grudge. But God's spirit softened my heart, and I knew I had to repent of my rage and forgive my mother's attacker. I wept and pleaded with God for the strength and will to forgive. God visited me in my closet and gave me a song, and it changed my heart. I began to pray for the man's health and well-being, and God continued to wash away my stubbornness and anger.
>
> Weeks later I saw the man on the street.
>
> My heart leapt with joy. I turned off my motorcycle and ran toward the man. He did not see me until I was upon him; he flinched and braced himself for a blow. Instead, he was wrapped in an embrace. "You are my brother. I love you," are the words that came from my

mouth. The man sputtered—confused—and then broke down in tears. We cried on the street as the man issued forth a stream of apologies and begged forgiveness. I granted it and insisted he come to my home and visit with my family. He obliged, and we dined together. We had peace and thanked God for healing. But that was not the end of the process.

Days later, I received a message from my mother: "You are no longer my son." My mother felt so betrayed by my forgiveness of her attacker that she could not eat. . . . Though my mother was a Christian, it took nearly two years for God to mend our broken relationship and make her understand his forgiveness.

Forgiveness is a messy business. I recently heard a preacher say that forgiveness is easy for Jesus. Though I think I know what he was trying to say, the truth is there is nothing easy about it. It cost him everything, his life. I've never heard a compelling story about forgiveness that was neat and tidy. But Jesus leaves us no choice. He commands us to forgive.

By refusing and clinging to our unforgiveness, we commit ourselves to carrying the pain of the past into the future. Lew Smedes wrote:

> The only way to heal the pain that will not heal itself is to forgive the person who hurt you. Forgiving stops the reruns of pain. Forgiving heals your memory as you change your memory's vision. When you release the wrongdoer from the wrong, you cut a malignant tumor out of your inner life. You set a prisoner free, but you discover that the real prisoner was yourself.

When we are forgiven by God, we receive grace, and when we choose to forgive someone else, we pour that same grace into their lives. By doing this repeatedly, we establish an economy of grace, the flow of God's grace through both lives, a dynamic that is both healing and transforming. The destructive effects of bitterness and unforgiveness are exchanged for the healthful effects of the forgiveness that is commanded in Scripture.

Think of the connections between forgiveness and health in some of the Old Testament descriptions of God's character. He is a God "who forgives all your sins and heals all your diseases" (Psalm 103:3), and when people turn from their sin, "then will I hear from heaven, and I will forgive their sin and will heal their land" (2 Chronicles 7:14).

If these ethical principles and commands, such as the command to forgive, are valid, they should both tell us something about our real condition, our humanity, and they should move us toward health and wholeness, helping us to function as we were intended to. They should keep us from harm. There are a number of dimensions of forgiveness to explore in relationship for their effect on mental and physical well-being—the ability to forgive oneself, to forgive others, and to experience forgiveness from God. And if we are correct in our assessment of the human condition and our need to forgive and be forgiven, we should not be surprised to learn that forgiveness is a key component of a healthy life.

Forgiveness and Health

There is some agreement among researchers that forgiveness consists of "giving up one's right to retribution and releasing or letting go of negative affect directed toward the offender," and that forgiveness must be distinguished from related concepts such as pardoning, condoning, excusing, and forgetting. Some studies emphasize how forgiveness operates, describing it as "a conscious, willful and moral act of embracing positive affect, behavior and cognitions toward a transgressor or life experience." And though forgiveness has been explored by psychologists since the 1980s, it is not an established mental health variable, and anger resulting from hurt, injustice, and unforgiveness has not yet found its way into the *Diagnostic and Statistical Manual of Mental Disorders* (DSM-IV). But it is clear that there is a lot of evidence connecting forgiveness to many aspects of health.

Across all age groups, forgiveness of self and others is associated with decreased psychological distress. Forgiveness leads to decreased depression and anxiety as well as a greater sense of satisfaction with life. Also, those who are engaged in learning how to forgive experience similar benefits.

For example, clinical evidence demonstrates that children can use forgiveness to lessen their anger resulting from disappointing relationships with parents as well as anger related to psychological disorders such as attention-deficit/hyperactivity disorder, oppositional defiant disorder, and others. Other studies suggest that forgiveness is associated with social competence, positive peer relations, and increased empathy.

Among college students, it has been shown that forgiveness leads to decreased anxiety and depression among those deprived of parental love, and decreased anxiety, anger, and grief in males upset by a partner's choice to have an abortion. Similar results have been discovered from researchers exploring self-forgiveness. Undergraduates who struggled to forgive themselves had greater levels of depression, anxiety, and neuroticism. In broad terms, young adults who forgive improve their global mental health, decrease stress, increase hope and optimism, improve relationship quality, and increase their sense of well-being. Forgiveness decreases levels of depression, stress, anger, social difficulties, and anxiety. Undergraduates who had difficulty letting go of anger directed at God experienced increased depression and anxiety.

And what about people nearing the end of their lives? One study focuses on the theoretical work of Erik Erikson and the final stage in Erikson's theory of life-span development, which involves the crisis of *integrity versus despair.* "If this stage is not resolved successfully, Erikson maintains that a person can slip into despair, which often involves 'fear of death.' " Pulitzer Prize–winning author and psychiatrist Robert Butler wrote that people spend a lot of time reviewing life in their later years, weaving their stories into a more coherent whole. "One of the key developmental tasks in the life-review process is the expiation of guilt, the resolution of intrapsychic conflicts, and the resolution of family relationships." If this is true, then one would expect matters like forgiveness by God and forgiveness of others to play an important role in lowering levels of anxiety about death. The findings of this study reveal that "older people who forgive others report that they experience fewer symptoms associated with a depressed affect than older people who are unwilling to forgive other people for things they have done." Also, older people who forgive tend to be more satisfied with their lives and are less anxious about dying.

In the area of physical health, there is mounting evidence that forgiveness protects people from heart disease and lowers blood pressure and heart rate. A recent study demonstrated that as patients learned to forgive there was a significant increase in blood flow within areas of the heart where blood flow had been impaired and tissue had been damaged by a heart attack. Also, forgiveness may have a role in recovery from cancer and can lead to a decrease in somatic pain. Another study showed a clear correlation between forgiveness and five measures of health—symptoms, number of medications, sleep quality, fatigue, and somatic complaints.

Many of the positive effects of forgiveness may be explained by the ways in which unforgiveness produces physical changes like those produced in other stress reactions. It can cause the kinds of hormonal patterns (especially glucocorticoid secretion), activities in the brain and nervous system, and blood chemistry changes that are consistent with stress and negative emotions. There is not sufficient evidence at this point to draw conclusions about the long-term effects of forgiveness on health. But it is clear that forgiveness is far more than a nice idea. It plays an important role in our physical and emotional well-being.

three

GRATITUDE AND HAPPINESS

Rejoice always, pray continually, give thanks in all
circumstances; for this is God's will for you in Christ Jesus.
(1 THESSALONIANS 5:16–18)

God commands us to "shout for joy," to "worship the Lord with gladness," to "enter his gates with thanksgiving," and to acknowledge that "the Lord is good" (Psalm 100). Paul wrote, "Rejoice in the Lord always. I will say it again: Rejoice! Let your gentleness be evident to all. The Lord is near. Do not be anxious about anything, but in every situation, by prayer and petition, with thanksgiving, present your requests to God" (Philippians 4:4–8).

A series of commands—Shout for joy! Worship! Be glad! Give thanks! Rejoice! Do not be anxious! Pray!

But how can gratitude and happiness be commanded?

It may seem to us that either we're happy or we're not and that if we're not feeling particularly grateful, there's nothing we can do about it. But the fact that these things can be commanded suggests that we can choose to be happy and grateful, that our will has an important role to play, that these are things that we do, in fact they are a way of life, more than they are things that we just happen to feel.

What Is Gratitude?

Paul traces the demise of the human race back to one specific aspect of our approach to God—ingratitude. "For although they knew God, they neither glorified him as God nor gave thanks to him" (Romans 1:21). Paul argues that out of this failure to understand the nature of our relationship to God, and the need to be grateful, grow all of the problems characterizing so much of life in the world today (see Romans 1:22–32).

In Deuteronomy 28, God warns of the fallout of human disobedience. But these problems are not only a consequence of their disobedience but also their attitude—"Because you did not serve the LORD your God joyfully and gladly in the time of prosperity" (v. 47).

Don't underestimate the power of the simple act of saying "thank you." We may not be fully aware of it, but when we say thank you and mean it—even in response to a simple kindness like passing the salt—we recognize that someone else had what we needed and graciously provided us with it. We express the positive emotions we feel in response to their kindness. These simple emotional exercises keep us tethered to a sense of reality, and without them we run the risk of missing so much of life's goodness and developing a sense of entitlement and independence. Gratitude is foundational to human relationships because it acknowledges our interdependence. It conveys to other people our appreciation for who they are, what they have done for us, and their participation in our lives.

Gratitude directed toward God is a measure of spiritual health in that it acknowledges that he is good and that we are utterly dependent on him. Part of living gratefully is being able to feel comfortable with our own neediness. The failure to feel and express appreciation reveals the core of the human condition. We no longer say "thank you" because we no longer feel our need. Dependence gives way to autonomy. We come to believe we can do it on our own.

Gratitude also means remembering the part we do not play in our well-being, in all of the things we cannot control. The health we experience, each breath we draw, our mind and abilities—all are gifts we receive from beyond ourselves.

When it seems appropriate, I sometimes suggest to those struggling with depression and discouragement that they list on paper all the things for which they are grateful. I have done this myself and find great comfort in it. Such lists are the source of many of the Psalms. The writer expresses a sense of need and recites God's provision for that need. In the same way, we can exclaim from the heart, "I know, God, that this is what *you* have done." Gratitude is where the soul's song of joy is born. Gratitude is a measure of maturity and is essential to a happy life.

What Do We Mean by *Happy*?

Feelings alone do not produce or explain happiness.

Again, it is surprising to realize that happiness is commanded (Psalm 66:1–2; Philippians 4:4; Romans 12:15; Luke 10:20). One contemporary writer has gone so far as to describe happiness as a "moral obligation." Joy is a winsome quality. We are by nature drawn to happy people. Happiness is a by-product of a life that is whole, purposeful, and invested in others and things that matter. The impact of our lives even within our families is shaped in significant part by our capacity for manifesting and expressing joy. Most of the time the most memorable qualities pointed out in eulogies are kindness and a capacity for joy and optimism. Happy people bless others and make the world a better place.

There is a lot of confusion about what happiness is, leading some people to prefer other words like *joy*. There is no simple definition. But it remains true that we all long to be happy. This is basic to our humanity. One of the simplest and truest confessions any person can make is that they want to be happy. Happiness, however we choose to describe it—a sense of well-being, peace, joy, blessedness, contentment—ought to be characteristic of life. There is nothing particularly virtuous or spiritual about dragging around in a state of gloom. Sadness and mourning may be necessary and appropriate for a season, but as G. K. Chesterton has said, "Melancholy should be an innocent interlude, a tender and fugitive frame of mind; praise should be the permanent pulsation of the soul. Pessimism is at best an emotional half-holiday; joy is the uproarious labour by which all things live." And I believe that joy to the world is still the perpetual desire of God's heart.

You and I were created for joy. The human heart is built in such a way that it hungers for the highest good for itself. By nature we seek happiness. Because of this, what we think will make us happy is a crucial factor in the shaping of our lives. Pascal wrote:

> All men seek happiness. There are no exceptions. However different the means they may employ, they all strive toward this goal. The reason why some go to war, and some do not is the same desire in both, but interpreted in two different ways. The will never takes the least step except to that end. This is the motive of every act of every man, including those who go and hang themselves.

William James drew the same conclusion:

> If we were to ask the question: "What is human life's chief concern?" one of the answers we should receive would be: "It is happiness." How to gain, how to keep, how to recover happiness, is in fact for most men at all times the secret motive of all they do, and of all they are willing to endure.

Our pursuit of happiness is rooted in the faculty of desire. Desire is a pervasive and inexorable component of our humanity. It seems at times to know no limits. And like the waters of a broken dam it rises, falls, and surges with enormous intensity. Desire animates us, drives us, overwhelms us, and shapes us. It accounts for the tremendous heaving and sighing of the whole of humanity. As Aristotle said, "It is the nature of desire not to be satisfied, and most [human beings] live only for the gratification of it." This aspect of our humanity exceeds the bounds of psychology. It is an expression of the spiritual component of self. And in a culture that tends to minimize the spiritual, we may run into trouble. When those spiritual yearnings that run deepest in the human spirit are not addressed in the course of day-to-day living, a huge and essential part of the joy of living can be lost.

Christianity is about life; not just quantity of life; i.e., eternal life, but also quality of life. The Christian life is more than a system of forgiveness that offers assurance about what will happen to us when we die. It is about how to live life now. And in the present moment it is about far more than how to live a morally correct life; it is about joy, fulfillment, meaning, and a sense of belonging. In the words of Jesus, he came that we might "have life, and have it to the full" (John 10:10; c.f. 7:38, 15:11).

But what about the whole spectrum of human experience? Life also brings with it much that does not, in itself, make for happiness. We cannot anticipate life's turns and the problems that may come. What about the pain, grief, loss, loneliness, and emptiness that are so much a part of the human experience? Even as I write it is not as if I can conceive of suffering as an outsider. I have seen more of death, discouragement, deprivation, and injustice, I have stood beside more hospital beds, buried more children, listened to more confessions, witnessed the shipwreck of more marriages and relationships, felt more of the hopelessness that comes with great loss and the pain of broken hearts than I can now remember or even care to remember. Years of involvement with people in the context of their struggles reminds me that our tremendous longing for happiness is often a far cry from the real experience of a durable joy.

Life *is* difficult and happiness does not mean that we are giddy, care-free, and cavalier. The good news of which Christians speak is not a means of blunting or redefining reality. It is not a quick fix. It is not pain free. There are no easy answers to life's problems. But there are answers.

I believe there is a way of life that faces difficulties realistically and responsibly, and that in this context we can experience the full-blown dimensions of life as it was meant to be lived—abundant, meaningful, and joyous. What we discover in the end is that happiness is a by-product of living a life that matters. We do this by finding out what matters to

God and digging ourselves deeply into those things. Happiness pursued as an end-in-itself will always elude us. But when our lives are shaped and defined by the gospel, and given over to God's purposes, the outcome is meaning, significance, and joy, even when the road is difficult.

Choosing Our Attitude

We cannot control our circumstances and the events of our lives, but we can choose the attitude we bring to those situations. Paul put it like this:

> Rejoice in the Lord always. I will say it again: Rejoice! Let your gentleness be evident to all. The Lord is near. Do not be anxious about anything, but in every situation, by prayer and petition, with thanksgiving, present your requests to God. And the peace of God, which transcends all understanding, will guard your hearts and your minds in Christ Jesus.
>
> Finally, brothers and sisters, whatever is true, whatever is noble, whatever is right, whatever is pure, whatever is lovely, whatever is admirable—if anything is excellent or praiseworthy—think about such things. Whatever you have learned or received or heard from me, or seen in me—put it into practice. And the God of peace will be with you. (Philippians 4:4–9)

Paul gives us several important directives on how to regain and keep perspective.

First of all, make the choice to rejoice and give thanks.

Second, practice preventative prayer. The typical pattern for prayer is that when we are faced with a problem, when we feel that things are out of control, we become anxious and we pray. First the problem, then the prayer. Paul, on the other hand, says that every day we are to give the whole of our lives to God in prayer before the problems come. Then we can realize that God is already there and involved in the situations we face even before we get there.

When I am preparing to see patients at the beginning of the day, I pray through my patient list and ask God to be in that room, involved in the encounter, and working for good. I pray that he would bring his power to bear on the needs of the patient and guide me in my words and decisions and the care I provide. When I walk into an exam room, I am aware that God is already there working. If I come to these situations with only my own ability to deal with things, I will be faced with anxiety. If at the outset of each day, I give everything to God—my wife and children, my work and encounters, my writing and sermon preparation, various pressures I face—if I invite him into all these places, I discover "the peace of God, which transcends all understanding."

Third, carefully choose what you think about. We really do get to choose. Referring to impure thoughts, Luther wrote that we cannot keep the birds from flying over our heads but we can keep them from building a nest in our hair. When we focus our thoughts on the true and the noble, the right and the pure, the lovely and the admirable, the excellent and the praiseworthy, we are creating an environment where God's peace can dominate.

Finally, Paul pushes us to emulate the habits of godly people, pointing the church at Philippi to his own example as a template for wise living, because such a life leads to peace of mind and peace in the lives of those around us. James put it like this:

> Do you want to be counted wise, to build a reputation for wisdom? Here's what you do: Live well, live wisely, live humbly. It's the way you live, not the way you talk, that counts. Mean-spirited ambition is not wisdom. Boasting that you are wise isn't wisdom. Twisting the truth to make yourself sound wise isn't wisdom. It's the furthest thing from wisdom—it's animal cunning, devilish conniving. Whenever you're trying to look better than others or get the better of others, things fall apart and everyone ends up at the others' throats.
>
> Real wisdom, God's wisdom, begins with a holy life and is characterized by loving others. It is gentle and reasonable, overflowing with mercy and blessings, not hot one day and cold the next, not two-faced. You can develop a healthy, robust community that lives right with God and enjoys its results only if you do the hard work of getting along with each other, treating each other with dignity and honor. (James 3:13–18 THE MESSAGE)

Anwar Sadat, the only Arab leader ever to address the Knesset in Israel, described this freedom to choose our attitude in his autobiography. He applied the lessons he had learned as a young man while a political prisoner in Cairo, applying them to the "huge wall of suspicion, fear, hate, and misunderstanding that has for so long existed between Israel and the Arabs." He writes,

> So I decided to look at the situation from a new angle and to embark on a fresh study that took all dimensions into consideration. . . . We had been accustomed (and a whole generation had been brought up) to regard Israel as taboo. . . . I concluded that any possible change should occur to the substance of that attitude itself . . . only thus, I decided, could we hope to break out of the vicious circle and avert the blind alley of the past.

My friend and counselor David Gatewood, when diagnosed with pancreatic cancer, said to me, "I want to live in such a way that will result in joy for the people I love." He fully accomplished this during two years of illness by continually maintaining an attitude of gratitude and hope even in a very difficult time. He died fully at peace with a smile on his face.

Happiness and Relationship

When we talk about living lives that matter by giving our time and attention to the things that matter to God, it is clear that according to Jesus these things are our relationship with God and our relationships with people (Matthew 22:34–40). It is remarkable how often Scripture connects these relationships with happiness.

Happiness in relationship with God—

- Splendor and majesty are before him; strength and joy are in his dwelling place. (1 Chronicles 16:27)

- You make known to me the path of life; you will fill me with joy in your presence, with eternal pleasures at your right hand. (Psalm 16:11)

- Surely you have granted him unending blessings and made him glad with the joy of your presence. (Psalm 21:6)

- Then I will go to the altar of God, to God, my joy and my delight. I will praise you with the lyre, O God, my God. (Psalm 43:4)

- Those the LORD has rescued will return. They will enter Zion with singing; everlasting joy will crown their heads. Gladness and joy will overtake them, and sorrow and sighing will flee away. (Isaiah 35:10; 51:11)

- Very truly I tell you, you will weep and mourn while the world rejoices. You will grieve, but your grief will turn to joy. (John 16:20)

- Though you have not seen him, you love him; and even though you do not see him now, you believe in him and are filled with an inexpressible and glorious joy. (1 Peter 1:8)

Happiness in relationship with each other—

- May your fountain be blessed, and may you rejoice in the wife of your youth. (Proverbs 5:18)

- In the midst of a very severe trial, their overflowing joy and their extreme poverty welled up in rich generosity. (2 Corinthians 8:2)

- Then make my joy complete by being like-minded, having the same love, being one in spirit and of one mind. (Philippians 2:2)

- Therefore, my brothers and sisters, you whom I love and long for, my joy and crown, stand firm in the Lord in this way, dear friends! (Philippians 4:1)

- For what is our hope, our joy, or the crown in which we will glory in the presence of our Lord Jesus when he comes? Is it not you? (1 Thessalonians 2:19)

- Your love has given me great joy and encouragement, because you, brother, have refreshed the hearts of the Lord's people. (Philemon 7)

- It has given me great joy to find some of your children walking in the truth, just as the Father commanded us. (2 John 4)

- I have no greater joy than to hear that my children are walking in the truth. (3 John 4)

- Rejoice with those who rejoice; mourn with those who mourn. (Romans 12:15)

Happiness and Learning

Happiness is also related to our capacity to learn and grow. This is not only a well established psychological principle but one expressed often in Scripture. James wrote, "Consider it pure joy, my brothers and sisters, whenever you face trials of many kinds, because you know that the testing of your faith develops perseverance. Let perseverance finish its work so that you may be mature and complete, not lacking anything" (James 1:2–4). In other words, problems can be a reason for joy if we recognize that one side effect can be spiritual growth.

Paul told us that in all things God works for the good of those who love him, who have been called according to his purpose (Romans 8:28). The argument is not that everything that happens to us is good. Some things are plainly rotten and evil; but Paul argues that God is big enough to cause all things to work out for some good in the long run for those who love him and are living according to his purpose. And the specific form of that good for Paul is anything that will help him "to be conformed to the likeness of his Son."

Enemies of Gratitude and Happiness

Losing perspective is easy. Like the first dent or scratch on a new car, sometimes the only thing we can see is the one thing that is wrong. We are rendered unable to see all the things that are right. Gratitude and happiness require an intentional choice to remember the good things.

There is perhaps no greater enemy of gratitude, and subsequently happiness, than comparing ourselves or our circumstances with others, what the Bible calls covetousness in the last of the Ten Commandments (Exodus 20:17). We are slow to compare ourselves with those less fortunate and easily see in others the things we think we don't have—the characteristics, physical attributes, experiences, relationships, possessions, and resources we feel we lack. We often do this without seeing the losses, hurts, and struggles in others' lives. Years ago, I was speaking to a group of singles about relationships, and I told them I grieved the lack of relationship with my father while growing up. A friend came up afterwards and stated that though she had a great relationship with her father, she was in her late thirties, single, had no children and no prospects of marriage, and that when she looks at my life all she sees are the things that I have. She gently reminded me that "we all have things in our lives we wish were different." Her wisdom was something I needed. Without this perspective it's easy to indulge in harmful ingratitude and unhappiness.

Our capacity for adaptation explains so much about our appetite for more—one more possession, one more experience. . . . And with this ability to adapt, a sense of entitlement can also creep in, causing us to feel that we have an inherent right to certain things. A subtle and insidious form of entitlement is simply taking the blessings of life for granted. Familiarity can be an enemy of joy. In marriage, familiarity can lead to the loss of the sense of the mystery and complexity of the other person, and ultimately a loss of wonder and respect. A good marriage involves looking over the edge, deep down into the soul of the other person every day. Familiarity can rob us of our sense of the miraculous and beautiful and dull our appreciation of life as a precious gift. Part of growing spiritually is unlearning our familiarity and experiencing again a childlike sense of wonder over everyday experiences. Gratitude produces mindfulness, awareness, intentionality, and joy.

Worry is another great robber. Worry over the past, our bursting schedules, and our focus on the future keep us from living fully in the present moment. The past is irretrievably gone. Tomorrow may never come for us. The only time we have to live is here and now, today. Paul encouraged us to let go of the past (Philippians 3:13). Jesus told us not to worry about tomorrow (Matthew 6:34). Now is the time and this is the place to learn to live in the kingdom of God, to fully appreciate the sanctity and preciousness of the gift of this moment.

The Benefits of Joy and Gratitude

The worst episode of depression I ever experienced arrived just in time for my first year of medical school. Carole and I were on our way to a wedding. It rolled in like a fog bank, and in minutes filled me with pain and confusion. I have a strong family history of depression. My parents had divorced a few months earlier, and our third child had just arrived. I was overwhelmed with life.

Medical school is a lousy place to be living in a mental and emotional fog. Though I was under the care of a good doctor, I found little relief. But during that year I developed a spiritual exercise that served me well and has continued to produce benefit and blessing. When I struggled emotionally, I would do three things that I could do in any setting and that would take me about twenty minutes.

First, I would ask God to show me any problems or burdens that were weighing on me, and whenever I identified one I gave it to God and asked him to carry it (Psalm 68:19; 1 Peter 5:7). Second, I would list in my mind all the things I had for which to be grateful. This is the heart of the exercise and takes the most time for me. Third, I would sing a praise song or recite a psalm of praise out loud or in my heart, depending on where I was. I cannot get through this simple process without something shifting inside me. I can't fully explain it, but without fail the darkness would lift and I would experience a lightness and peace that would allow me to get unstuck and keep moving forward.

I not only survived that first year, but laid a good foundation academically, saw my marriage and relationships with my children grow, and experienced greater confidence in God. After twelve months, the depression lifted as quickly as it had come, and thankfully to this day it has never returned to that degree.

Gratitude, which is also commanded, has a measurable positive effect on our mental and physical well-being and is crucial to spiritual health as well. There is growing empirical evidence that gratitude is an important aspect of healthy relationships, mental health, and well-being. Research suggests that grateful people are more energetic, optimistic, resilient, healthy, compassionate, helpful, and satisfied with life. They also suffer less depression and are less materialistic. In general, they have a greater sense of well-being. Grateful people are happier people.

Gratitude is also connected to relationship. People who feel a sense of connection with other people are more likely to feel grateful to God. Spiritually or religiously inclined people are more likely to experience gratitude and the physical benefits of gratitude.

When it comes to our physical health, an analysis and summary of thirty studies on happiness and longevity indicates that happiness leads to a longer life. This is especially true among healthy populations. A summary of nineteen follow-up studies observed the same positive effects of happiness on longevity, stating that they are "quite sizeable" and amount to as much as ten years. Some of the factors contributing to this increased longevity are that chronic unhappiness increases stress and leads to higher blood pressure and a weakened immune response. Happy people, on the other hand, are more inclined to healthful behavior like watching their weight and participating in physical activity, are more able to cope with adverse circumstances, and in general make better choices in life. The study suggests an interesting implication for preventative healthcare, "that we can make people healthier by making them happier."

My dear friend Dr. Robert Meye, the former dean of the School of Theology at Fuller Seminary, wrote a letter to the *LA Times* regarding the ongoing discussion at the time about "what to do about" Terri Schiavo, a young woman with severe brain damage whose life became a matter of national discussion and debate. Dr. Meye wrote,

> I have lived by a feeding tube for the last ten and a half years. For more than a decade I have not eaten so much as a crumb of bread or drunk a drop of water. I am totally dependent upon the feeding tube inserted into my stomach for my daily food and drink.
>
> By now you know something about feeding tubes; on television

everyone has seen Terri Schiavo's uncovered stomach, with a feeding tube leading into it. Well, that's just about the way I look . . .

As I faced surgery in 1994, a panel of surgeons reviewed my case. One of them, I understand, saw no point to a (second—and there would be a third) big surgery for oral cancer at that point, feeling that the quality of life beyond surgery did not support surgical intervention. Well, here I am, a decade later, having lived a good, full decade, and having traveled the world in the meantime.

On one expedition, I had my picture taken in front of the stunning snow-covered Matterhorn in Switzerland holding high in my left (my right side is partially disabled) hand one of the 7 or 8 cans of food that would flow through a feeding tube into my stomach that day. We enlarged that picture to poster size and gave it the caption "Quality of Life" and consigned it to the doctor who did not want to consign me to life with a feeding tube.

Now, what's my point? My point is that there is life beyond the feeding tube. In my case, lots of life. To be sure, my life is cluttered up with all kinds of problems, large and small, but not one of them—nor all of them taken together—even comes close to robbing me of the great joy of living.

So what does this have to do with Terri? Well, obviously, she too lives by the feeding tube, and she too has had life beyond the feeding tube. To be sure, it has been a horribly diminished life—but nonetheless life . . .

I say, let Terri live. Give her the same food and drink that we all need—including me, through my feeding tube. There is life beyond the feeding tube—all kinds of life.

Dr. Meye is a man who faces life as well as devastating illness with great energy and courage. His happiness and sense of gratitude have served him well and challenge me in my attitude in far smaller challenges in my life. A few months ago, I visited him in the ICU of a local hospital after another surgical intervention. Some had little hope for his recovery. A few weeks later, I saw him at the funeral of a dear friend a hundred miles north of here in Santa Barbara, to which he had driven himself along with his wife. He continues to persist in his belief that life is a wonderful gift.

Jessica Mastan is another hero of sheer joyful confidence in God. When Jessie was twelve, persistent pain after a fall while playing soccer led to an MRI revealing a mass in her hip. In the days that followed she was diagnosed with Ewing's sarcoma, a rare and very aggressive form of bone cancer. After five months, when chemotherapy failed to eradicate the cancer, Jessie and her parents were faced with a very difficult choice.

I remember Jessie as a three-year-old, with her soft curls and porcelain complexion, wearing a burgundy velvet dress, with all the imagined characteristics of an angelic being and a heart and spirit to match. That little girl quickly grew into an impressive athlete. She loved motion: running, sprinting, swimming, basketball, soccer, and dance. Now she was faced with the choice between a debilitating surgery and certain death. Jesse faced that choice with unflinching courage.

Her father, Dave, described to me his feelings the day of the surgery as they arrived at the hospital in early morning darkness. He dropped off Jessie and her mother, Cathleen, at the front door before parking, and Dave recalled the painful realization as he watched Jessie walk away from the car toward the entry door of the hospital that this might be the last time he saw his daughter walk.

That day in surgery Jessie had fully half of her pelvic bone removed. For many people, such a surgery means that they will never walk again or that they will need assistance to walk for the rest of their lives.

For six weeks after the surgery, Jessie was in a brace that kept her body straight while she healed. Any trips to the hospital involved an ambulance and a stretcher. A good friend of the family, Dan, who is a mechanical engineer, designed and constructed a ramp providing access to the front door.

Jessie faced the challenge of walking again like all the other challenges she faced—with courage and tenacity. She often commented that because of people's prayers she had suffered so much less than many others suffer during chemotherapy and stem cell transplant. She beat the world record for the recovery period and went home from the hospital after seventeen days. She was told that it would take at least a year to learn to walk again, and then only with a walker. In less than six months, Jessie was walking again without assistance.

Months after this, Dave suggested to Jessie that they ought to tear the ramp down. They agreed that it was time. Dave explained to me that the ramp in the front of the house had become for him the constant reminder and unavoidable symbol of all the losses their daughter had experienced. According to Dave, Jessie had found the grace to embrace and accept her condition while he had mustered only an eighty or ninety percent acceptance, and the cumulative effect of those small percentages over time had produced a great deal of frustration.

One Saturday morning, Dave armed himself and his daughter with hammers, a crowbar, and a determined attitude. They were ready to go. Dave explained to Jessie that this was a chance to take out some anger, to reach way down inside and tap into her frustration, to gain a measure of control over what had become the symbol of an uncontrollable life change. Jessie took a few big swings with the hammer, but didn't do any real damage. Dave told her to get angry, projecting his own feelings onto the situation. But Jessie just looked at him, and with a sweet smile and the courageous heart that characterized her, she simply said, "Daddy, I'm just not angry." She set down her hammer and walked up the ramp and into the house.

One of the things that always struck me was the sense of normalcy she conveyed whenever I saw her even in difficult situations, no matter how hard things were. For Jessie, her response to illness and life-threatening disease was not special—it was simply the choice people make to live with gratitude and joy every day.

Earlier this year, at the age of fourteen, Jessie died as the result of a massive stroke. The message of her life was amplified by her death because she refused to be defined by a disease or to allow difficult circumstances to rob her of the joy of living.

Every one of us is faced with such choices every day—choices about our attitude, whether or not to be grateful, choices to live as happy, joy-filled people.

PART 2:

Instructions for Our Relationships With Others

four

SEX

Flee from sexual immorality.
All other sins a man commits are outside his body,
but he who sins sexually sins against his own body.
(1 CORINTHIANS 6:18)

The Simple Truth

We live in a culture deluged by sex—television shows and commercials with constant references to sexual behavior, music videos averaging more than ninety sexual situations per hour, graphic pictures easily accessed on the Internet designed to attract teenagers—all producing a distorted sense of sex and what is normal and healthy.

The biblical teaching on God's design for our sexuality is simple and unambiguous.

Sex is a gift. God created us as sexual beings, with a sexual identity, and with a capacity for sexual relationships (Genesis 2:7, 18–25). Sex is intended for our pleasure, as we see it celebrated in the Song of Songs with its joy, playfulness, eroticism, and ecstasy. It is also intended to be an expression of love and joy-filled commitment, a commitment that is potentially costly and enduring, lasting a lifetime. It contributes to a sense of connection and investment, providing a means of bonding and experiencing deep intimacy with another person as we join body and spirit. It allows us to give a part of ourselves to another person. It brings with it the possibility of producing children and all the responsibilities that come with them.

Sex was made for marriage—one man and woman in a relationship built on mutual love and respect, rooted in lifetime commitment expressing the character and sacrifice of Jesus (Genesis 2:24; Matthew 19:4–6; Ephesians 5:21–23). All other relational expressions of our sexuality outside of this context are described by the Bible as sin or sexual immorality and are to be avoided (Exodus 20:14; 1 Corinthians 5:9; 10:8; Galatians 5:19; Ephesians 5:3; Colossians 3:5; 1Thessalonians 4:3–8; Hebrews 12:16; 1 Peter 2:11; 2 Peter 2:13–14; Revelation 21:8).

There are many reasons marriage is the only "safe" place where our sexuality may be expressed. The misuse of our sexuality has damaging effects on us and those around us physically, emotionally, and spiritually. The fallout of the misuse of human sexuality is immense—sexual addiction, pornography, unwanted pregnancy, abortion, physical and emotional post-abortion complications, disease, destroyed relationships and marriages, emotional damage, loss of wholeness, prostitution, trafficking and abuse of women and children, personal guilt, shame, and much more.

The Fallout

Physically, the misuse of our sexuality puts us at risk for infectious diseases including gonorrhea, Chlamydia, syphilis, human papilloma virus, herpes simplex virus, HIV, and others. It is not an exaggeration to say that a single generation of compliance with simple biblical guidelines regarding sex, as unrealistic as that may seem to some, would lead to the near eradication of sexually transmitted diseases.

Emotionally, the act of sex is unlike most physical acts in terms of the complex impact it has on us when misused. It leads to shame, guilt, emotional risk and losses, and other costs that cannot be calculated up front. Sex can be a powerful force in destroying people. The horrifying reality of the molestation of children, or the rape of women, make it clear that there is no greater abuse, and there are no deeper wounds than the ones that come through sexual violations. But even without the violence, abuse, and manipulation involved in such acts, we cannot overlook the pain, damage, and sense of betrayal caused by sexual infidelity, or the kind of emotional loss that comes when sex is detached from commitment and responsibility.

The corrosive effects of the misuse of sex can be witnessed in the people engaged for years in prostitution. In my previous book, I told the story of a young man named Anthony, a patient I met at a county hospital years ago who deeply impacted my attitudes and my life. At seventeen, he had spent several years on the street as a prostitute. He had already experienced terrific losses—the loss of home and relationship with his parents, the loss of health to HIV and AIDS, the loss of hope to what he saw as the irreversible course of his life, and the loss of peace to guilt and shame.

Some people may question the validity and necessity of his guilt and shame, viewing them as an unnecessary consequence of the manipulation of religion. I would argue that there is a kind of guilt that we all experience that is instinctive and inescapable, rooted in our innate knowledge of who God is and what he is like (Romans 1:19–21).

Anthony described to me a life filled with loneliness, hopelessness, and pain. No one would be able to convince Anthony that the way he used his sexuality produced anything but harm. But he was eventually transformed by the good news that God loved him so much that Jesus made the choice to live and die to set him free. Anthony died about a year later at peace, knowing he was loved and full of hope because of this good news.

Part of the corrosive effect of the misuse of sex is because sex also affects us *spiritually*. Paul explained:

The body, however, is not meant for sexual immorality but for the Lord, and the Lord for the body. By his power God raised the Lord from the dead, and he will raise us also. Do you not know that your bodies are members of Christ himself? Shall I then take the members of Christ and unite them with a prostitute? Never! Do you not know that he who unites himself with a prostitute is one with her in body? For it is said, "The two will become one flesh." But whoever is united with the Lord is one with him in spirit. Flee from sexual immorality. All other sins a man commits are outside his body, but whoever sins sexually sins against their own body. Do you not know that your bodies are temples of the Holy Spirit, who is in you, whom you have received from God? You are not your own; you were bought at a price. Therefore honor God with your bodies. (1 Corinthians 6:13–20)

Many yearnings of the human soul are ultimately spiritual. When answers to our spiritual longings are not found in the course of our day-to-day lives, we may find ourselves seeking answers in all the wrong places. Sex involves becoming "one flesh," a unique expression of solidarity and connectedness, as we use our bodies to act out our deep longing for connection, meaning, and intimacy. We express with our bodies what is going on in our spirits. God created Adam's body and breathed into him the breath of life. Our bodies and souls are deeply connected. M. Scott Peck writes that those lost in a compulsive pursuit of sex are in fact looking for spirituality. Malcolm Muggeridge describes sex as the mysticism of the materialist. G. K. Chesterton said that "every man who knocks on the door of a brothel is actually looking for God."

While all sin is more than a merely physical act, since it affects us spiritually, sexual sin is unique because of the spiritual union that occurs. Without the commitment of marriage, it can tear away pieces of ourselves that are essential to our well-being. It's like ripping a pocket from a shirt—the damage is greater than we intended or anticipated. We lose a little bit of ourselves every time we misuse our sexuality, and the injury and pain that occur leave us with an inescapable sense of guilt, remorse, and shame.

Paul makes another strong statement explaining the effects of sexual sin:

> Therefore God gave them over in the sinful desires of their hearts to sexual impurity for *the degrading of their bodies* with one another. They exchanged the truth about God for a lie, and worshiped and served created things rather than the Creator—who is forever praised. Amen. Because of this, God gave them over to shameful lusts. Even their women exchanged natural relations for unnatural ones. In the same way the men also abandoned natural relations with women and were inflamed with lust for one another. Men committed indecent acts with other men, and *received in themselves the due penalty for their error.* (Romans 1:24–27)

Like all sins and addictive attachments, sexual sins bring with them their own punishments and negative effects.

But sexual purity involves more than just avoiding intercourse outside of marriage. The problem is not just homosexuality and adultery and a select list of concerns. Jesus said, "You have heard that it was said, 'Do not commit adultery.' But I tell you that anyone who looks at a woman lustfully has already committed adultery with her in his heart" (Matthew 5:27–28). In other words, lust is one of those sins that damages us on its way out of our hearts.

> What comes out of a person is what defiles them. For it is from within, out of a person's heart, that evil thoughts come—sexual immorality, theft, murder, adultery, greed, malice, deceit, lewdness, envy, slander, arrogance and folly. All these evils come from inside and defile a person. (Mark 7:20–23)

Every one of us is broken by the effects of sin, and that brokenness includes our sexuality. There is no room for a sense of moral superiority or self-righteousness that would cause us to look down our noses at others who are struggling.

Sexual sin has adverse effects, but we must remember that we are not saved by sexual purity any more than we are saved by any other human action. We can only be saved because of what Jesus has done for us. A relationship with Jesus through which grace is poured into our lives is the beginning of the healing and wholeness we need. For sex to take on a proper proportion in our culture and in each of our lives, we must learn that a huge part of the connectedness we long for is found in a relationship with Jesus, the God who made us. And as he heals, we discover love and meaningful connections in healthy, interdependent relationships with family and friends and, often, in marriage. In the context of marriage, which is an act of the will in which we choose to love someone else with the same commitment with which God has loved us, sex finds its only healthy, life-giving expression.

What Science Tells Us

With all the intentional efforts to avoid judgmental language in scientific literature, it is a bit surprising to find so much written that is so negative about the causes and effects of sexual promiscuity.

One of the most thoroughly studied topics regarding sex outside of marriage is the effect of cohabitation on relationship success. I define love, based on a broad understanding of Scripture, as a commitment of the will and a joy of the spirit resulting in choices to act in the best interest of the one loved. The biblical description of marriage emphasizes the importance of commitment, specifically the commitment of marriage, as the proper context for sex. One of the things to emerge from these studies is the importance of commitment to long-term relationship. Cohabitation "sabotages" the success of these relationships. Living together before marriage had a significant negative effect on both the stability and quality of the marriages studied. Cohabitating couples who eventually married experienced higher levels of instability and disagreement, decreased interaction, lower marital satisfaction, less supportive behavior, less time spent together in shared activities, less positive problem solving, more marital problems, less effective communication, and an increased likelihood of divorce. And cohabiting couples had a five times greater rate of separation than married couples.

The reasons teenagers become sexually active are important to understand as one step in addressing the situation. Some of the more common reasons include peer pressure, a desire for connection, an attempt to flag and keep the attention of a partner, media influence, and a negative self-image, to name some of the most common. For each of these reasons and others, adults can take steps that grow out of committed love, care, and attention, which can help teenagers move toward responsible and healthful choices (more about this in the next chapter).

Teenagers are far more likely than adults to engage in unprotected sex. Some estimates suggest that half of people infected with HIV each year are in their early teens to early twenties. Sexually active teenagers are also more prone to depression and suicide. Risky behaviors are increasingly understood as the cause of depression rather than a symptom of depression.

Ignoring the limits God has placed on the use of our sexuality comes at a high price. Our culture is drowning in the fallout of the misuse of sex. But today you can choose to do things God's way. Save the gift of your sexuality for marriage. If you're in a relationship where you are sexually active and not married, ask God to help you reshape that relationship in the way that he desires. That's what's best for everyone involved. Wherever you may struggle with sexual sin, call out to God and ask him to help you move away from sin and toward healing and wholeness. If you are feeling the guilt, pain, and loss of a soul that has been shredded by sexual sin, call out to Jesus. He can reweave the torn emotional fabric. He will forgive and make you whole, someone new.

A New Start

The most moving experience I have ever had participating in a baptism occurred about twelve years ago. A young woman in her mid-twenties who wore unusually revealing attire started coming to church. After a few weeks she began bringing a friend who shared a similar taste in fashion. Then several months later, she made an appointment with me at the church office.

This young woman had the drawn, hardened look of someone who had had a hard life. She shared with me that she had worked for a number of years as a prostitute and stripper but could no longer go on as she had, feeling guilty and hopeless about the future. She felt she had ruined her life. As a child she'd had a dose of religion, which contributed to her sense that what she was doing was wrong. She started coming to church because she wanted a different life, and then had prayed in one of our services, giving her life to Jesus. She wanted to know where to go from there.

She continued to grow. Her dress and appearance changed, but more important, she was clearly becoming a different, happier person from the inside out. When she was baptized about six months later, she exhibited a joy and emotion I have never seen in that setting before or since. About a half hour before the baptism she began crying tears of unspeakable joy over how Jesus had loved her and made her someone new, a different person. She cried through her testimony and while she was being baptized and long afterwards. She was simply amazed by grace.

She is now happily married to a man who adores her, and together they have a daughter. She is a godly woman, continuously learning and growing and looking more like Jesus all the time. She ministers to women with problems like the ones God brought her through, and she would tell you that Jesus not only forgave her but invited her to sin no more, to live a different life (John 8:11–12). Every time I see her I feel a renewed sense of hope about what God is doing in the world.

five

LOVE, COMMITMENT, AND FAMILY

Husbands, love your wives and do not be harsh with them.
Children, obey your parents in everything, for this pleases the
Lord. Fathers, do not embitter your children,
or they will become discouraged.
(COLOSSIANS 3:19–21)

Last week I went to the courthouse with some friends for the finalization
of their adoption. Tiffany has lived with John and Diane for over a year.
At fourteen she has faced truckloads of pain and unpredictability. But all
of that changed last week as the court made permanent and legally binding
the commitment they had already made in their hearts. They were each
questioned by the judge about their intention, then they each signed papers
describing their choice to be a family. Through tears the judge explained
that they were now parents and child just as certainly as if she had been
born their biological child. She said that not everything was going to be
perfect and easy, and that there was still a lot of hard work ahead to resolve
the inevitable conflicts and maintain love and good communication.

Watching all of this tapped into some deep feelings in me. It was hard
to grasp how an act of choosing could be so transforming. Adoption is

proof that love is thicker than blood, commitment more important than biology, and grace greater than anything in our past.

Sometimes people try to tell us that Ciara was fortunate to find a home and family like ours. I reflexively feel a bit confused. I think I know what they are trying to say. Two doctors told us that Ciara never would have made it through her first year without the level of care we were able to give her. But the truth is, we're the blessed ones. She has brought far more to our lives than we will ever bring to hers.

Jonathan is our firstborn. I remember with vivid images the moment he was born—the head crowning, revealing curly dark hair, the way he seemed to slip into this world. Tears poured out as I was overwhelmed by feelings of expansive joy, but mostly love—the kind of unexplainable love that overwhelms and sits on your chest, the kind of love that makes you willing to die for someone. I've never stopped loving Jonathan like that. He's nineteen now. We have been through some of the messy parts of growing up, the discipline, arguments, battles for control. He recently told us we had it really easy as parents. *You should see what my friends put their parents through.* The man that has emerged is strong and beautiful. He's crazy in love with Jesus. As I write, he is in Iraq on a mission project, teaching English and learning Muslim culture. Right now I feel all the same things I felt at the moment he was born. He's our son, a precious gift entrusted to us by God for a brief while. One day, soon after he was born, I came home from work to find Carole crying, really crying. She was holding Jonathan. I asked her what was wrong and she said, "He's so precious, so precious."

That same amazing process repeated itself with the birth of Caitlin and Brendan. We have also been through the birth of two children whom we were adopting. When Aaron was born, and later at Ciara's birth, we were overwhelmed all over again. I felt that same love. I could hardly stand it, I felt so full. The truth is I loved them before they were born. Even though Carole didn't "carry them," we were expecting them, carrying them in our hearts and investing emotionally, committing to them long before they arrived. It reminds me of the way God loves us—the way he knows us before we have a physical existence, the way he anticipates our life by creating scrapbooks about us before we exist as a single cell (Jeremiah 1:5; Psalm 139:15–16).

This kind of love is a strange thing. Most of the loves in life are learned and developed. I fell in love with Carole in the process of learning about her, and I have other friends I learned to love over time. But love for one's children is something different. It seizes you, overwhelms you. In the hospital, I have met a lot of people, people like me, potentially self-centered and self-serving, who would gladly give up everything for their children—sleep, comfort, money, jobs, everything—out of the hope that their children might get well.

Love and Commitment

At the heart of Christianity is the message called the *gospel*. This good news, the best possible news, is the only message that offers an answer to the human dilemma—God loves us so much that he himself comes to rescue us from all the things that would destroy us. It is a story of relentless love. God chooses us, makes us his children, shows us his commitment and faithfulness. The ethics of life in the kingdom of God grow out of the simple choice to love people the way we have been loved by God.

But what is love? What does God's love look like? In the previous chapter on sex, I explained it like this: Love is a commitment of the will and a joy of the spirit that expresses itself in the choice to act in the best interest of the beloved.

This definition has three parts. Each part is essential.

First of all, to understand the love of God, we must understand that God's love is rooted in commitment. God's love expressed through a human life is characterized by the same kind of patience and faithfulness that he shows to us. Its limits are not dictated by emotions. We walk into a new relationship optimistic, full of trust and hope about the other person, but we soon find that they also have problems and struggles. The relationship becomes more costly and difficult than we anticipated. *Agape* is a love that persists when the going gets tough, when it's not easy to love.

To say that love is a commitment of the will does not mean it is void of emotion. For love is also a joy of the spirit. There's a gladness, goodness, gleefulness to love. Much of the time loving is something we want to do because of the value we place on the beloved.

These foundational aspects of love consistently lead us to choose to act in the best interests of our loved ones. Love is practical. It makes the choice to serve.

Taken together, these three ideas—commitment, joy, and service—form a basic working definition of godly love.

Commitment. Commitment is foundational to an adequate understanding of God's love, agape. Paul emphasized this commitment in his definition of love in 1 Corinthians 13: "Love knows no limit to its endurance, no end to its trust, no fading of its hope; it can outlast anything. It is, in fact, the one thing that still stands when all else has fallen" (vv. 7–8 J.B. PHILLIPS TRANS-LATION). Love is not fickle; it is not mere sentimentality; it is not subjective; and it is more than a nice feeling. Love is concrete and practical because it is rooted and grounded in the character of God. God is love. When we talk about genuine love, we must always realize that we are talking about what God is like. God's love is a love that never gives up on us. The Old Testament word for God's love requires more than one English word to convey its meaning—it is covenant love, committed love, faithful love.

When Jesus wanted to reveal his Father's heart toward sinners, he told a story about a son who ran away from home, squandered the family's wealth, and dishonored his father. The portrayal of God as a father who waits, day after day, night after night, watching from the window, looking out with longing, desiring his son to come home—this is a picture of the loyalty and fidelity of God's love. And when that son finally did come home, his father's love was still intact. The father's love never depended on the behavior of the son. It was always about who the father was. This is the nature of God's love for us. He never gives up on us. In fact, such relentless commitment is the hallmark of his love, and the foundation of all such committed loves. The no-matter-what commitment of Christ to the church anticipates the commitment of marriage, and the no-matter-what commitment of our heavenly Father to each of us, his children, models the commitment of a parent to a child.

Joy. Though commitment is foundational, love is more than commitment. In its various expressions, love is often characterized by joy—the mystery and excitement of romance, the playfulness and intensity of sexuality, the goodness of friendship, the warmth of familial love. Love is a breathtaking dance between joy and commitment, play and discipline, freedom and resolve, ecstasy and agony. This is the model of all loves from the greatest Lover: "For the *joy* set before him he *endured the cross*" (Hebrews 12:2).

Service. Love causes us to act in the best interest of others, which means that it has a protective effect on those around us, our relationships. This is why we say that love fulfills the law, or does everything that the law demands.

Every law is given for one of three reasons: to protect our relationship with God, to protect our relationships with other people, or to keep us safe spiritually. God gives us the law as a guardrail to keep us from plunging over the edge into disaster. It functions positively and graciously in preventing sin-damaged people from doing further damage to themselves and their relationships.

> You, my brothers and sisters, were called to be free. But do not use your freedom to indulge the flesh; rather, serve one another in love. The entire law is fulfilled in keeping this one command: "Love your neighbor as yourself" (Galatians 5:13–14).

> Let no debt remain outstanding, except the continuing debt to love one another, for whoever loves others has fulfilled the law. The commandments, "You shall not commit adultery," "You shall not murder," "You shall not steal," "You shall not covet," and whatever other commandment there may be, are summed up in this one command: "Love your neighbor as yourself." Love does no harm to a neighbor. Therefore love is the fulfillment of the law. (Romans 13:8–10)

> One of them, an expert in the law, tested him with this question: "Teacher, which is the greatest commandment in the Law?" Jesus replied:

" 'Love the Lord your God with all your heart and with all your soul and with all your mind.' This is the first and greatest commandment. And the second is like it: 'Love your neighbor as yourself.' All the Law and the Prophets hang on these two commandments" (Matthew 22:35–40).

When love is functioning well in a human life, when you love other people as God loves them, love fulfills all of the law, because both the law and love are expressions of God's righteousness, justice, and mercy. It is not possible to passively express the righteousness and justice of God. There is more to fulfilling the law than avoiding hurtful behavior. Love not only avoids harming its neighbor, it discharges every debt. Loving others involves the choice to "serve one another in love" and to love others the way we want to be loved ourselves. God's love erases the imaginary line between the sacred and the secular so that Christian freedom involves moving beyond a life in a cordoned-off area defined by the law, into the joy of moving through the whole world, guided by a heart transformed by the love of God.

What Happened to Commitment?

A culture's character can be measured by where it finds itself along a continuum of *commitment* on one end and *abandonment* on the other.

Commitment ——————————————————— Abandonment

What is our commitment as a society to the well-being of children, to the lives of children not yet born, and to the elderly? Where are we in our response to the needs of our own children and our responsibilities as fathers and mothers? What about the health of our marriages and our faithfulness to them, our willingness to give them the time and attention they need? Would we rather live together without the commitment of marriage? What about other abandoning activities by which we evade responsible behavior, such as drug abuse, crime, infidelity, child abandonment, and abortion?

The alternative to commitment, a preoccupation with self, is the emotional milieu that drives so much of our culture today. When God is displaced from his rightful place in the human soul, other gods are waiting to move in. Often the most convenient substitute is simply ourselves. First published about thirty years ago, *Psychology as Religion: The Cult of Self-Worship* by Paul Vitz is one of the most important books I've read describing the spirit of our age. Vitz writes that the religion of our day is "self-ism," which is the measure of the universe and the world as it affects *me.* Though psychological insight can provide tremendous benefit, without a proper context it can be detrimental, adding to our confusion. Vitz argues that for many, "Psychology has become a religion, in particular, a form of secular humanism based on worship of the self."

What does this mean for relationships? It means that as long as a relationship is serving our interests, keeping us happy and entertained, then we'll stick with it. But when that relationship no longer satisfies our needs and makes us happy, we'll get rid of it, because we are the center of the universe. For many, this is the religion of the day. Its consequences are devastating. Vitz writes:

> For selfists there seem to be no acceptable duties, denials, inhibitions or restraints. Instead, there are only rights and opportunities for change. An overwhelming number of selfists assume that there is no unvarying moral or interpersonal relationships, no permanent aspects to individuals. All is written in sand by a self in flux.

Dietrich Bonhoeffer, the great German pastor and theologian, was imprisoned for his opposition to the Nazis and his involvement in a plot to assassinate Hitler. He remained in prison until he was hanged days before the end of World War II. He wrote many letters later compiled in a book. One of these messages was to his nephew, written on the eve of the nephew's wedding, "A Wedding Sermon from a Prison Cell." It contains an amazing statement about the nature of married love:

> In your love you see only the heaven of your own happiness, but in marriage you are placed at a post of responsibility towards the world

and mankind. Your love is your own private possession, but marriage is more than something personal—it is a status, an office. Just as it is the crown, and not merely the will to rule, that makes the king, so it is marriage, and not merely your love for each other, that joins you together in the sight of God and man. . . . *It is not your love that sustains the marriage, but from now on, the marriage that sustains your love.*

Bonhoeffer understood that love is ultimately about commitment. It's not warm feelings that sustain the relationship; it's the ongoing choice we make to stay together through thick and thin.

Jacob's love for Rachel is described in what I consider the most romantic verse in the Bible: "So Jacob served seven years to get Rachel, but they seemed like only a few days to him because of his love for her" (Genesis 29:20). That's God's kind of love—joy and passion mixed with commitment and hard work.

The best definition of married love I've ever read came from a woman who had been married for twenty-seven years and had raised six children with her husband. She said, "Love is what you've been through with somebody." Love isn't meant to last only a few months or years, then fade away. It is meant for a lifetime. Love becomes more fully itself only in the long haul. Without going through the middle and doing the hard work of figuring out what it means to form a life together, without having a partnership that endures difficult times and celebrates life's good gifts, we miss the blessing of moving from the emotional place where a marriage begins to the deep and wonderful place where a marriage can find itself later in life. Commitment is the glue that holds our lives together and causes us to stay the course.

Without such commitment, our lives are written in sand, and the only thing that can change this is the committed love of someone else. Lew Smedes, in a sermon, once said this about marriage:

> But what a mysterious, what a wonderful thing to do! Only some-one in the image of God could do it—could say to anyone when you don't know what the future is going to be, and you don't know how much you are going to change, and you don't know how much the

other person is going to change, still to say, "I am the one who will be there with you." To reach out into a future you don't know and say, "This one thing you can know—I'll be there with you." To stretch yourself out and make a rendezvous with someone in circumstances you cannot control and say, "This one thing you can control—I'm the one who will be there with you."

To create an island of certainty for someone in the midst of an ocean of uncertainty—to create an enclave where this one thing is predictable, your presence and your caring. To dare to make and care to keep a commitment. When you do that and when I do that we are more like God than we are at any other time.

Belonging

Commitment is important because we all need to belong somewhere to someone. We long to be connected. It's how we are made. I have met people who feel they have no one. A friend of mine grew up without a father, was alienated from her mother for decades before her mother died, has no siblings, no aunts, uncles, or cousins, no one who is family in any traditional sense. She is single and old enough that she is convinced she will never marry, never have children. I have also felt the loss and loneliness of children growing up without their fathers, children growing up in foster care, children who have lost their only parent to death. Such losses are crushing. We need to belong.

God wants us in relationship, to belong to someone, to sense that we are loved, not only by him but by people who value us and are committed to our well-being.

> A father to the fatherless, a defender of widows,
> is God in his holy dwelling.
> God sets the lonely in families,
> he leads out the prisoners with singing. (Psalm 68:5–6)

When my relationship with my father seemed irreparably damaged, there were men who took me under their arm and loved me and gave me the nurture and direction I desperately needed. Long before I was a biological father, I had parental responsibilities as God brought children into my life who needed the same things. In the kingdom of God we are all family, we are all mothers and fathers, we all have a responsibility to address the needs of the next generation.

There is a great need today for people who are willing to offer love that can be counted on—that is, the very love of God. Such committed love provides security and stability that can help us become the people God created us to be. This kind of love has the power to lower our defenses, move us toward deeper relationship and connection, and with time, invite healing.

Commitment and Marriage

The positive effects of committed love, expressed over time, on physical health and emotional well-being are well documented.

The converse of this reality can be seen in the physical effects of divorce, which can lead to increased risk of diabetes, some forms of cancer, heart disease, depression, Alzheimer's disease, and other illnesses. In fact, married men live about ten years longer than those who are divorced. The effects of divorce on life expectancy appear to be the result of the multiple stressful transitions involved—the termination of relationships, decreased involvement with children and other family members, disapproval from others, loneliness, isolation, and the loss of social support. Divorce is also associated with a decrease in healthy behaviors, increased smoking and alcohol consumption, heavier use of medication, and decreased physical activity.

But we must be careful when talking about statistics. When we talk about divorced people, children with divorced parents, and children who grow up without their fathers, we are talking about people, individuals— some of whom have suffered terribly—who need respect, understanding, and support. It is important to remember that every person is different in their experiences and responses, and that statistics should not be generalized to individuals. People need understanding, not presumption. Just because there are tendencies within these groups does not mean that an individual will suffer inevitable outcomes. We have choices, unique temperaments, resources, and access to God's grace.

And I would not pretend to be able to judge people who are divorced or understand their circumstances or experiences. At the same time we need to try to understand the effect of these trends within our culture, precisely because they do affect people. There is an ocean of pain pouring out of the epidemic of divorce.

The impact of divorce on children has been carefully studied, and it indicates that the breakdown of the family has placed children at great risk. More than half of the children of divorce will have no contact with non-custodial fathers. They have a significantly increased risk of emotional and behavioral problems, depression, suicide, and alcohol and substance abuse. They suffer academic setbacks including an increased rate of dropout, lower test scores, and lower grades. They are more prone to earlier sexual activity and multiple sexual partners, increasing their risk of sexually transmitted infections, cervical cancer, and pregnancy. They have shorter life spans.

Many of these effects may be best explained by the stress placed upon the child—the stress of change, loss of attachment, fear (particularly fear of abandonment), and hostility between parents. Elizabeth Marquardt explains in *Between Two Worlds: The Inner Lives of Children of Divorce* that marriage provides a singular world in which parents seek to reconcile differences. Divorce creates two worlds and places upon the child the impossible task of reconciling and making sense of the increasingly divergent worlds of their mother and father.

Marquardt points out that the preponderance of divorce literature is written by and for divorced adults and tends to tell them what they want to hear. This leads to a lot of "happy talk" about divorce aimed at helping parents alleviate guilt. "But when divorce happy talk minimizes, distorts, or ignores the pain felt by children of divorce, it crosses over into the realm of harm." Her book is based upon retrospective methodology, including interviews and a national survey of young adults from intact and divorced families asked to look back on their childhood. She argues that the truth about the impact of divorce on children is found in listening to the voices of the children of divorce. The problem with the happy talk is that it lies to children. It treats life after divorce as a fun adventure, whereas children typically experience painful losses, moral confusion, spiritual suffering, broken relationships, and increased risks for all kinds of problems.

The stress of divorce carries over into adult life. About one-third of children whose parents remarried after divorce indicate that they found the remarriage more stressful than the divorce. When the children's relationships with their fathers deteriorated after divorce, so did their relationships with paternal relatives, including grandparents. Parental conflict adds stress and threatens a child's well-being by creating worry that their parents will no longer care for them. This loss of well-being has measureable effects on physical health. Those impacted by divorce are more likely to postpone marriage or not marry at all, and those who do marry are more likely to divorce.

Commitment and Parenting

The more elaborate the organism, the longer it depends on its parents. A housefly has no period of dependence, a sparrow two weeks, a squirrel two months, and a human being about eighteen to thirty years.

For humans, this is reflected in the fact that our brains are not fully developed at birth. Myelination—the formation of an insulating material around the *axon* of a *neuron*, which is a specialized cell within the nervous system—is essential to smooth the flow of brain impulses necessary for the successful development of cognitive, motor, and sensory functions. This process requires at least ten to twelve years but may continue into adolescence and possibly even adult life.

The importance of family to a child's well-being is reflected in this long period of dependence on one's parents. The basic needs of children include not only food and shelter, but consistent love and acceptance, the establishment of basic trust, relational skills and socialization, direction and discipline, the learning of values, the development of language, and the skills necessary for healthy living and functioning in the world.

The Bible is clear about the importance of family and the obligation of a husband and wife to love each other as well as their children. For example, there is an emphasis in the book of Proverbs on direction and discipline:

> Start children off on the way they should go,
> and even when they are old they will not turn from it.
> (Proverbs 22:6)

There are also instructions in the Law for parents to teach their children their history as God's people and the Law itself:

> Fix these words of mine in your hearts and minds; tie them as symbols on your hands and bind them on your foreheads. Teach them to your children, talking about them when you sit at home and when you walk along the road, when you lie down and when you get up. Write them on the doorframes of your houses and on your gates. (Deuteronomy 11:18–20)

Another reminder of the infinite value of every child is the care extended to children by Jesus, including his assertion that children reflect the character of those who live in the kingdom of God (Matthew 18:1–5).

Science continually reinforces the benefits of commitment of parents toward their children and consistent time spent with them. One important study, the *National Longitudinal Study on Adolescent Health,* reported that parent-family connectedness and a feeling of positive connections at school were protective against every health risk behavior measured except history of pregnancy. Parental expectations regarding school achievement were associated with lower levels of health risk behaviors, and parental disapproval of early sexual debut was associated with a later age of onset of intercourse. Parent-family connectedness was generally defined as "the presence of parents at key times during the day (at waking, after school, at dinner, and at bedtime), shared activities with parents, and high parental expectations for their child's school achievement."

With notable consistency across the domains of risk, the role of parents and family in shaping the health of adolescents is evident. While not surprising, the protective role that perceived parental expectations play regarding adolescents' school attainment emerges as an important recurring correlate of health and healthy behavior. Likewise, while physical presence of a parent in the home at key times reduces risk (and especially substance use), it is consistently less significant than parental connectedness (e.g., feelings of warmth, love, and caring from parents).

A more recent survey of developments in literature regarding parenting practices and adolescent development draws similar conclusions:

Recent scholarship demonstrates the significant, enduring, and protective influence of positive parenting practices on adolescent development. In particular, parental monitoring, open parent-child communication, supervision, and high quality of the parent-child relationship deter involvement in high-risk behavior. Authoritative parenting generally leads to the best outcomes for teens. . . . Authoritative parenting . . . is characterized by a high degree of warmth and support, firm limit setting, open communication, and high levels of supervision. . . .

It is not just the commitment of parent to child that counts, but the commitment of parents to each other. For example, a study of cohabiting parents looked at maternal depression and sensitivity to children, and found that cohabiting mothers experienced more depression and were less sensitive with their children than married mothers. These differences appeared to be explained in part by the observation that the cohabiting relationships were characterized by more ambivalence and conflict.

Fatherlessness

We are now facing the needs of what has become known as "the fatherless generation." Their stories are woven into the fabric of our culture through songs, movies, books, and blogs, and all too often theirs are stories of shattered dreams, lost potential, emotional pain, and loss.

Forty percent of all households in the United States are single-parent households, and this number jumps to 80 percent for African-American homes. Two out of every five children in the U.S. do not live with their fathers. While divorce is a major factor, the rise of fatherlessness began with the increase of single teenage mothers in the sixties. There are many contributing factors, including imprisonment, death, abandoning behaviors, irresponsibility, and laws that sometimes fail to acknowledge the importance of a father's connection with his child.

The statistics about the effects of fatherlessness are disturbing. Sixty-three percent of youth suicides are children from fatherless homes. Eighty-five percent of the youth in prison grew up in fatherless homes. Girls who grow up without their father are at greater risk for early sexual activity and teenage pregnancy.

Research also reveals the role of the absence of a father in the development of masculinity in boys and femininity in girls, in academic achievement, in moral development, in incarceration rates, and in the development of psychological disorders. One researcher summarizes the findings:

> This area of research broadly and conclusively suggests the detriment of a father's absence to the development of both girls and boys. For example . . . adolescents who had experienced father loss or absence were two times as likely to drop out of school, 2.5 times as likely to become teenage mothers, and 1.4 times as likely to be out of school or work.

Another researcher wrote,

> Fatherlessness is the most harmful demographic trend in this generation. It is the leading cause of declining child well-being in our society. It is also the engine driving our most urgent social problems . . . if this trend continues, fatherlessness is likely to change the shape of our society.

What we are faced with is far more significant than merely a bunch of statistics. We are talking about an epidemic chewing at the soul of our culture, leading to children who are often marginalized or ignored, faced with pain, loneliness, and isolation, frequently lacking the love, nurture, and guidance they need. As American culture becomes increasingly matriarchal in the home, school, church, and workplace, as marriage gives way to cohabitation, as the ultimate right of passage for masculinity—fatherhood—is increasingly challenged by divorce, unwed parenthood, poor role models, and the failure to grasp the importance of the father's role in a child's development, one has to wonder what the future holds for males in our culture and how big the problem must become before we recognize the desperate reality that our shift in values has created.

What can easily be missed is the importance of a father in a daughter's life. His kind words, respect, and affirmation of her beauty can help her see that her life is important and meaningful, which profoundly impacts her identity and character. One research project seeks to quantify "father hunger," the longing of children for connection with a father. For daughters, this sense of need may drive them to find comfort in relationships with men that prove destructive.

True religion responds to human need, especially in the most vulnerable. The Bible is filled with tough-minded statements about the needs of the widow and the fatherless. These people are our responsibility (Deuteronomy 10:18; 14:29; 16:11–14; 24:19; Isaiah 1:17, 23; 9:17; Jeremiah 7:5–7; James 1:27).

Jesus often used the phrase "the least of these" to describe the helpless, the powerless, the unimportant in the world's eyes, the poor, people whose needs will only be addressed when we dare to believe that everyone is important and matters to God. "See that you do not despise one of these little ones. For I tell you that their angels in heaven always see the face of my Father in heaven . . ." (Matthew 18:10–14). These little ones matter to God. They have their own angels who continually gaze upon the face of God. In our eyes they may seem unimportant, but in God's eyes they have infinite value and importance.

I'm not an engineer, but as I understand it, most filtration systems involve a series of filters—the first in the series gets the big chunks and the last one catches the finest particles. People who follow Jesus are God's finest filter—the last line of protection for the little ones, the least of these, children, widows, the poor, the sick, and the homeless. We must keep them from being ignored, forgotten, unloved, or from simply falling through the cracks. Our world is in need of such a filter.

The problem of fatherlessness presents a serious challenge to the church. The church is to be a counterculture within the culture—not separate from it—working for the common good of the culture. I agree with Ernest Becker's suggestion that if Christian people would take their own message and values seriously, demonstrating a willingness to act on what they believe, to act as though the truth were true, the tide could turn.

How can Christians respond in a way that makes a difference?

I think it has to begin with a shift of focus from our own interests to the interests of others, a commitment to the well-being of the next generation. It is not likely that this need will be met by churches that place their own traditions, worship style, and preferences above the well-being of youth, or by churches that have lost their theological moorings, that have given up on the gospel for a more popular message, and who are no longer able to offer biblical hope. Churches must be able to offer a heroic alternative to the materialism, hedonism, and narcissism of our culture, not merely the hope of the "American dream"—living in a nice middle-class neighborhood, raising nice middle-class children, having plenty of comfort and nice things, ignoring the needs around us. This approach to life fails to speak to the wounds on the souls of so many younger people today.

By and large, churches tend to be segregated, not just along racial lines, but also by age. Many churches provide multiple worship experiences separated by age-group, so that much of our worship is no longer multigenerational. In order to help the fatherless, we need to cross generational lines. The answers to people's needs will not be found in well-crafted statements but in strategic action and committed love.

One key way we can express this love and turn the tide is to connect young men to godly older men through intergenerational mentoring relationships in which the older man pours into the life of the younger wisdom, guidance, and care, modeling what it is to be a man and providing a sense of connection and belonging.

That love will be expressed in a growing concern for those in foster care and those who need to be adopted. In the United States, there are always about 130,000 children awaiting adoption. Thirty percent of these children have been in foster care for more than two years. Most will age out of the system when they turn eighteen, never knowing the consistent love of a family. At Bethany, the church where I serve, we have made these children a high priority, facilitating programs directed at their needs, resulting in an inordinate number of adoptions within our church family and significant impact on the community regarding this issue. It is no irony that our children's ministry director is an adoption attorney as well.

My own lack of connection to my father left me empty, lonely, confused, afraid of men my father's age, and uncertain of myself and my abilities. I felt solidly on the path to nowhere. Some of the men of the church I now pastor took me under their wing and helped guide me into manhood. They loved me, disciplined me, and showed me the ropes. A critical moment in my development came when my mother suggested I visit a godly man who lived across the street from the public high school I attended. Jim McReynolds was a quadriplegic as the result of polio he contracted in the 1950s. From a wheelchair he was a husband and father, raised eight amazing kids, preached regularly at prisons and rescue missions, taught Bible studies, and mentored many young men. He died when I was a freshman in college. Of the six guys he was discipling at the time of his death, all of us ended up in full-time ministry. Thank God for Mel Friesen, Paul Byer, Colin Brown, and others who followed up the work Jim began. Healing has come slowly, but without their help I cannot see how it would have come at all.

I pastored a church not too far from Bethany for eight years before medical school and residency. When I started medical school, we came back to Bethany, where I had met Carole when we were teenagers, and where we both grew up. The church was having problems, and I helped fill in when the pastor left. The very men who had raised me spiritually saw in me the competency to lead. They insisted I pray about it, and one thing led to another. The office where I am working right now is the office where, as a nine-year-old, I prayed with the pastor and gave my life to Christ. That pastor, Dr. Bob Shaper, one of my mentors, not only led me to Christ but also taught my preaching courses in seminary, preached and laid hands on me at my ordination, did our premarital counseling, led us in our wedding vows, and dedicated each of our children.

Dr. Shaper died last year after a five-year battle with Alzheimer's disease. On our last visit, I asked him if he knew who I was. He could not remember my name, but he said, "I do know you. You are the one who keeps showing up." When I was leaving, I said to him, "Remember, we are in this together." He responded by saying, "Isn't that something? To have someone who is in it with you."

Another key step in turning the tide involves widening our circle of inclusion and making these at-risk children a part of our families— the very thing God has done for us. As we identify these children in our neighborhoods, we can choose to develop relationships with them, have them over for dinner, and include them in our youth groups, family vacations, holiday celebrations, and trips to Disneyland. We can let them know they are one of us—that they are welcome to hang out and to become a real part of the family.

Henri Nouwen saw the church as a host whose function is to invite people in. The difficult part of such ministry is that if we are too full of ourselves and our own plans, we cannot pay attention to our guests. We must be ready to let go of our own agendas and expectations. We don't know what our guests will bring to the mix, what baggage they carry, or how disruptive we may find them.

The fulfillment of our commission requires us to invite people into our lives or to invite ourselves into the lives of others, as Jesus often did. The most loving thing we can do is invite other people to come and meet Jesus and his people.

Rebecca Pippert, in her book *Out of the Salt Shaker and into the World*, told the story of her arrival in Portland, Oregon, in the '70s, where she met

Bill, a student at one of the campuses where she served. He was a brilliant but disheveled young man with messy hair, and she recalls that she never saw him in a pair of shoes. Bill became a Christian, and one day decided to attend a middle-class church across the street from the campus. He walked into this church of well-dressed people in his worn jeans, T-shirt, and bare feet. People looked uncomfortable, but no one said anything as Bill walked down the aisle looking for a seat. The church was filled, and as he came to the front pew, without hesitation, he sat down on the carpet in the middle of the aisle, casually crossed his legs, and waited for the service to begin. The tension mounted as people stared. Then a well-respected man in his eighties began walking down the aisle toward the student. People whispered their concerns, anticipating the scolding that was coming. *Well, you can't exactly blame him for scolding the guy . . . he is being disruptive.* As the old man approached Bill, the church was quiet. All eyes were glued front and center to see what was going to happen next. With some difficulty, the old man lowered himself to the floor and sat down next to Bill. He crossed his legs, and the two of them worshiped together on the floor.

Turning the tide on our cultural drift away from the needs of children will require humility, commitment, and the ability to see others as more important than ourselves. The utilitarian approach that views children as inconvenient, and their needs as unimportant, has caused a wound and is killing their hearts.

Young and old alike are hungry for kindness. Kind people harness God's power in their actions and words. They are agents of transformation. Most of the time people cannot hear the Christian message until they see it in a human life. They will not recognize us as followers of Jesus until we love them the way he does. Kindness causes hearts to open and words to take on increased value. Our actions begin to tell the story of God's kindness, and if our words are also motivated by love, our message takes on tremendous integrity.

It's not enough to tell people that God loves them. They need to see that love acting through us. They need to know that we love them. The choice is ours.

PART 3:

Directions for a Healthier Self

six

SELF-CARE: HEALTH AND WELLNESS

Do you not know that your bodies are temples of the Holy
Spirit, who is in you, whom you have received from God?
You are not your own; you were bought at a price.
Therefore honor God with your bodies.
(1 CORINTHIANS 6:19–20)

When I look at a patient, I have intentionally learned to see more than
a physical body and its physiology. I see someone infinitely and wonderfully complex—capable of love and relationship, language and creativity,
great good and great evil, deep feelings, emotional needs and longings,
spiritual appetite, a longing for that "something more"—a mortal miracle.
This perspective keeps us mindful that there is more to health than the
maintenance of a body, that health is a complicated phenomenon involving the whole person.

Our bodies are not incidental to our humanity. Genesis tells us that
in a deeply personal creative act—in the way an artist shapes a work of
art—God formed a human body. The rest of creation is spoken into existence, but human beings are shaped by God's hands as it were. Describing

the event poetically, James Weldon Johnson (1871–1938) captures the love and intimacy involved in creating a human being.

> Up from the bed of the river
> God scooped the clay;
> And by the bank of the river
> He kneeled him down;
> And there the great God Almighty
> Who lit the sun and fixed it in the sky,
> Who flung the stars to the most far corner of the night,
> Who rounded the earth in the middle of his hand;
> This great God,
> Like a mammy bending over her baby,
> Kneeled down in the dust
> Toiling over a lump of clay
> Till He shaped it in his own image;
>
> Then into it He blew the breath of life,
> And man became a living soul.

In the same way Jesus, who often conveyed healing by speaking the word, healed a leper by laying hold of him, by touching someone considered unclean, untouchable. Jesus assumes our humanity, and while living with us as one of us was known as a "friend of sinners." There is no part of being human about which God is sheepish, with which he is not willing to engage.

At the same time, we are more than a physical body. Genesis 2 also tells us that God breathed into the man the "breath of life," pointing to an immaterial part of our humanity, a soul.

Our bodies help us experience the world, express emotions, worship, and act upon our thoughts. They are created to allow us to interact with the physical and spiritual dimensions of reality.

The psalmist wrote,

> I have seen you in the sanctuary
> and beheld your power and your glory.

Because your love is better than life,
my lips will glorify you.
I will praise you as long as I live,
and in your name I will lift up my hands.
My soul will be satisfied as with the richest of foods;
with singing lips my mouth will praise you. (Psalm 63:2–5)

In worshiping God, the psalmist employs his physicality (eyes, lips, hands, posture, voice), his emotions (love, praise, desire), and his spirit (in praising and glorifying God and experiencing the satisfaction of his soul). The same language used to describe our encounter with physical things is used to describe our encounter with God. All of this—mind, body, emotions, and spirit—make us who we are. Jesus drew a distinction between the body and soul: "Do not be afraid of those who kill the body but cannot kill the soul . . ." (Matthew 10:28). Augustine described human makeup like this: "But the soul is present as a whole not only in the entire mass of the body, but also in every least part of the body as well."

While some people insist that only the soul matters, others claim that we are no more than a biological entity. Cognitive science and neuroscience have revealed changes in metabolism and function in parts of the brain in relationship to activities like religious thought, prayer, and worship. Some conclude that the spirit is no more than a function of the brain. The fact that brain function and metabolism are affected by spiritual behavior can just as well be explained by the possibility that the body and spirit are inextricably connected. What is the mind? What is spirit? Is there some part of our consciousness and experience of being that exists apart from the material brain? What is the relationship between consciousness and the function of the brain? Unquestionably there is a pervasive interdependence between our consciousness and experience of the world and what is happening in our brains. But the idea that the spirit is merely a function of the brain cannot be established scientifically. Some argue that because we have some understanding of the neurobiological processes involved in choice, for example, that there are no deeper, spiritual processes at work. But the exquisite complexity of brain processes and the unpredictability introduced by environmental influences on the brain call for a great deal of humility regarding what we actually know at this time.

We are complex beings, and recognition of this fact is foundational to a way of life leading to health and wholeness.

Amy Carmichael was born and raised in Northern Ireland, and as a teenager in Belfast began to throw herself into work helping the poor. She eventually went to India in 1895, where she remained for fifty-five years, without leaving, until her death. She settled in Southern India, in Dohnavur, where she discovered the practice of "dedicating" children to Hindu temples. Many girls were sold as temple prostitutes, married to the gods and available to the men who visited the temples. As a result of this practice, thousands of infants were born in desperate need of being rescued. Amy began a work devoted to saving "temple children." She was charged with criminal kidnapping and often threatened with violence, but hundreds of children were rescued. She was mother, doctor, and nurse, twenty-four seven. She became known as *Amma* ("mother" in Tamil). The physical needs she faced were severe and demanding. When criticized for doing social work and not evangelism, for saving bodies and not souls, she responded: "Souls are more or less securely attached to bodies . . . and as you cannot get the souls out and deal with them separately, you have to take them both together."

Wholeness

Nature displays expressions of life's limits. Fallen trees and leaves, the fading beauty of the flower, and the scars and lines that mark our bodies are all reminders of our mortality. This awareness, the ability to know "the number of my days," and "how fleeting my life is," is an aspect of wisdom (Psalm 39:4). We are "wasting away," but our hope is that "the one who raised the Lord Jesus from the dead will also raise us with Jesus" (2 Corinthians 4:13–16). But having this hope for the future does not allow us to ignore our health today. And taking care of ourselves involves more than just taking care of our bodies.

On one occasion some Pharisees observed Jesus' disciples eating food in the marketplace without the ceremonial washing prescribed by the elders. The Pharisees asked Jesus why his disciples ignored the tradition and ate with "defiled hands." Jesus replied:

> "Nothing outside a person can defile them by going into them. Rather, it is what comes out of a person that defiles them."
> After he had left the crowd and entered the house, his disciples asked him about this parable. "Are you so dull?" he asked. "Don't you see that nothing that enters a person from the outside can defile them? For it doesn't go into their heart but into their stomach, and then out of the body." (In saying this, Jesus declared all foods clean.)
> He went on: "What comes out of a person is what defiles them. For it is from within, out of a person's heart, that evil thoughts come—sexual immorality, theft, murder, adultery, greed, malice, deceit, lewdness, envy, slander, arrogance and folly. All these evils come from inside and defile a person" (Mark 7:15–23).

Paul touched upon the same truth when he wrote,

> For physical training is of some value, but godliness has value for all things, holding promise for both the present life and the life to come. (1 Timothy 4:8)

Jesus is not saying that it doesn't matter what we put in our bodies. Paul is not saying that exercise is unimportant. They are both saying that there are things that can absolutely and ultimately destroy us, and that addressing these things will have great benefit now and eternally.

We are complex beings. The biblical and holistic view of humanity describes physical, mental, emotional, and spiritual dimensions. This is reflected in the greatest commandment to love God with our whole being—heart, soul, and body (Deuteronomy 6:5). The goal of the pursuit of health and healing is more than the health of our bodies and is really a pursuit of wholeness or wellness. A physician who forgets this matter of human complexity reduces his or her role from healer to mechanic.

Sin and the Body

Sin is a core issue in health and wellness. It leads to self-damaging behavior, while godliness leads to healthful choices. Sin has a negative impact on us, the people around us, our feelings about ourselves, and our environment. And it affects us at multiple levels. Most illnesses and diseases grow out of a multi-hit process. There is more than one factor leading to them, and these factors may derive from more than one aspect of our humanity.

For example, we may be too busy because we are compensating for our fear of death and our need to prove ourselves. We eat poorly, lose sleep, deplete our emotional reserves, and encounter a virus. Our body is not fully prepared to resist, and so we get a cold. A single illness may grow out of physical, emotional, and spiritual issues.

There is growing evidence that cancer is a multi-hit phenomenon requiring the accumulation of multiple genetic changes. These changes are associated with aging, chronic tissue damage, chronic inflammation or infections, the effects of cell damaging substances, chromosomal translocations, and inherited genetic abnormalities. The onset of cancer is a complex process, as these factors and others cause changes within or around the gene. Likewise, the development of coronary artery disease may involve stress, poor diet, and genetics.

But this connection between body and spirit works both ways. The physical can impact us emotionally and spiritually. For example, if bypass surgery is required because of heart disease, the trauma to the body often produces a profound depression.

The connections between body and soul are also clearly seen in drug abuse and addiction. The effects of drug abuse are wide-ranging, such as loss of appetite, lack of motivation, confusion, impulsivity, depression, anxiety, and dangerous behavior. A psychologist friend often argues that all drug addicted patients are, in fact, depressed.

Many physical and emotional problems are amplified at the end of life. Often the experience of terminal illness raises issues of pain and comfort, loneliness and isolation, regret, family issues, depression, and questions about the meaning of life.

Again, health is far more than a purely physical issue. Understanding this can help us appreciate more fully what is involved in taking steps toward health and wholeness.

But not everything is within our power. When we talk about health, we are usually talking about those matters over which we sense some control. While we shouldn't minimize the importance of doing what we can to maintain health, the truth is there is so much of life over which we have no control. The onset of many illnesses, such as muscular dystrophy and certain types of cancer, cannot be prevented. We can eat well and exercise, but there are factors of physiology, genetics, the environment, and other variables over which we have no control. They have nothing to do with decisions we have made. Diet and exercise books are popular in part because they point to things we can control. But those who would try to convince us that almost all disease is preventable not only fail to recognize our limitations, but may cause us to blame ourselves for things that we can't control.

Our daughter Ciara has cerebral palsy and a seizure disorder, likely the result of poor medical management at birth. We were there for her birth, but as adoptive parents we had no say in her care, and from the womb she had no control over circumstances that will impact her for the rest of her life.

Spiritual Wellness

There is a connection between the body, emotions, and spirit, and understanding each of these aspects of our humanity can help us move toward health and wholeness.

As creatures created by God in the image of God, no factor is as important to our well-being as our relationship with God. That relationship, whatever it may be, even if we don't believe in God, impacts us profoundly.

When we know God, he can lift from our shoulders the burden of guilt and shame. He can help us know who we are and understand the purpose of our lives. He provides the grace needed for emotional healing and the forgiveness of others. He provides wisdom that is foundational to making sound choices about how to live. He places us in a family where we can find the love and support we need (Psalm 68:5–6). Our only hope of spiritual wholeness is in relationship with God. He leads us to a way of life that is truly life-giving (Proverbs 6:23; 8:35; 11:30; 21:21).

There is a growing interest in the impact of religious involvement on health, and research consistently indicates that such involvement increases life expectancy. In the many studies reviewed in the Oxford University Press *Handbook of Religion and Health,* religious faith has generally increased happiness, hope, optimism, coping, marital stability, and sense of purpose, while decreasing depression, anxiety, suicide, and drug and alcohol abuse. One doctor summarizes the literature by saying that "weekly attendance at religious services accounts for an additional 2 to 3 life-years compared with 3 to 5 life-years for physical exercise and 2.5 to 3.5 life-years for statin-type agents [cholesterol drugs] . . . and rough estimates even suggest that religious attendance may be more cost-effective than statins."

Emotional Wellness

Sin harms us emotionally. Genesis tells us that the consequence of sin is guilt and shame. It makes us want to hide and cover our nakedness, blaming others for our condition and pretending to be someone other than who we are (Genesis 3:7–13).

The choice of positive thoughts and emotions, and the rejection of toxic thoughts and emotions have a profound impact on our health. Viktor Frankl discovered in the darkness of Auschwitz that prisoners like himself who could focus on a reason to live and maintain hope were much more likely to survive. He explains:

> In spite of all the enforced physical and mental primitiveness of life in a concentration camp, it was possible for spiritual life to

deepen. . . . Only in this way can one explain the apparent paradox that some prisoners of a less hardy makeup often seemed to survive camp life better than did those of a robust nature. In order to make myself clear, I am forced to fall back on personal experience. Let me tell what happened on those early mornings, when we had to march to our work site.

There were shouted commands: "Detachment, forward march! Left–2–3–4! Left–2–3–4! Left–2–3–4! First man about, left and left and left and left! Caps off!" . . . Whoever did not march smartly got a kick. . . .

We stumbled on in the darkness, over big stones and through large puddles, along the one road leading from the camp. . . . Hiding his mouth behind his upturned collar, the man marching next to me whispered suddenly: "If our wives could see us now! I do hope they are better off in their camps and don't know what is happening to us."

That brought thoughts of my own wife to mind. And we stumbled on for miles, slipping on icy spots, supporting each other time and again, dragging one another up and onward, nothing was said, but we both knew: each of us was thinking of his wife. . . .

For the first time in my life I saw the truth as it was set into song by so many poets, proclaimed as the final wisdom by so many thinkers . . . that love is the ultimate and the highest goal to which man can aspire. . . . The *salvation of man is through love and in love.* I understand how a man who has nothing left in this world still may know bliss, be it only for a brief moment, in the contemplation of his beloved.

We saw in chapter 3 the way in which the apostle Paul spelled out the components of a healthful perspective: Make the choice to be grateful and joyful. Give the whole of your life to God in prayer every day. Focus on the good. Follow the example of godly people (Philippians 4:4–8). The result is peace, which will contribute to increased physical wellness.

Many have faced traumatic events or emotionally damaging experiences and deeply feel the need for healing. When Jesus touched a leper, befriended sinners, cried at the death of his friend, and welcomed women and children, he demonstrated both his power to heal and his awareness of the vastness of human need. Emotional and physical healing go hand-in-hand. Through Jesus' life we witness the power of the Holy Spirit to reweave the emotional fabric torn in our hearts and to love us in a way that leads us to trust him, a trust that is foundational to health and a sense of well-being. Today that healing may come through us—the expression of kindness, meeting a physical need, caring friendship, a time of prayer, the help of a gifted counselor, and in many other ways.

The prevalence of depression is on the rise. Some of the depression we experience is a normal part of living—a response to grief, pain, and loss. Major depression is a clinical term involving symptoms such as depressed mood, sadness, tearfulness, loss of interest, motivation, or pleasure, feelings of guilt or low self-worth, poor sleep, loss of appetite, low energy, and the inability to concentrate. This condition can become chronic and deeply impair one's ability to negotiate the routines and responsibilities of everyday life. For many, these symptoms may be so severe that they lead to suicide, the tragic cause of the loss of about 850,000 lives each year.

Depression is the leading cause of disability and a leading contributor to the global burden of disease. By the year 2020, it will be ranked second as a contributor to global disease according to the World Health Organization. Depression affects about 120 million people worldwide. Only about a third of these people seek treatment and only 25 percent have access to effective treatment.

Depression is a beast that can chew up a life. It should be taken seriously by the struggling individual as well as his family, friends, and medical providers. Patients should be carefully examined and evaluated for illnesses like low thyroid production and other conditions that can cause fatigue and depression. Sometimes depression is a symptom of an underlying medical problem. Effective treatments include several kinds of therapy, and medication has also been shown to be effective, especially for people with severe depression. A combination of therapy and medication appears to be most effective for adolescents.

Unfortunately, there is a tendency today to just throw medicine at depression as a means of avoiding the complex and possibly time-consuming issues involved in its care and treatment. Consideration should be given to supplementing medical care with other means of support—talking with a friend, competent counseling, consistent prayer, a team of supportive people, exercise, and time outdoors. If a doctor does not instruct a depressed patient who is physically able to take long walks out in the sunshine, they may be neglecting important aspects of care.

Depression is at least in part a physical problem. There are physical differences in the brains of depressed people, involving the number and distribution of receptors involved in feelings of pleasure and well-being. I bring this up because of my concern over religious people who view depression as a purely spiritual issue, rejecting the potential benefits of therapy or medication, causing people who need such help to feel unspiritual, which can sometimes lead to disastrous consequences.

Physical Wellness

My intention in this section is not to provide comprehensive guidance on nutrition, exercise, or particular health problems, but simply to provide a framework that might help shape our ideas about health, encouraging people to focus on some of the relevant issues. There are several factors over which we have some choice. And when given a choice, we can usually reason our way to the most healthful options by thinking about the way God intends things to be.

At the end of Deuteronomy, the last of the books of the law, we find the song of Moses, in which he recounts God's faithfulness and provision for his people. He reflects on the experience of Jacob during his sojourn:

> The LORD alone led him;
> no foreign god was with him.
> He made him ride on the heights of the land
> and fed him with the fruit of the fields.
> He nourished him with honey from the rock,
> and with oil from the flinty crag,
> with curds and milk from herd and flock
> and with fattened lambs and goats,

with choice rams of Bashan
and the finest kernels of wheat.
You drank the foaming blood of the grape.
(Deuteronomy 32:12–14)

It is God who provides food to nourish us, to provide energy for the things he asks of us. In the area of nutrition, we face a lot of choices not only about the quantity of food we consume but also its quality. We benefit by choosing foods that are as close to nature as possible, in other words, closest to the way God made them, paying attention to how they are produced. Food that is organic and unaltered is almost always healthier. Try to avoid fast food, processed food, food stripped of nutrients, and chemical-laden foods. The foods listed in the Bible are simple foods found in nature, not things that are changed and processed. These natural foods are filled with nutrients essential to health. The use of some fertilizers, feed products, drugs, and genetic alterations aimed at increased food production can be a blessing at one level, but may also bring unintended consequences.

Emphasize fruits, vegetables, whole grain, and nuts, all of which are sadly lacking in the Western diet. The whole and less-processed foods are usually found around the perimeter of the store. Select high quality protein sources, organically produced when possible, and avoid unhealthy fats. And keep well-hydrated.

When it comes to exercise, technology has reduced the effort required to survive. Cars have eliminated much of our walking, our work is done in a chair at a computer, and our hours are filled with television instead of activity. Our way of life no longer provides the exertion and strengthening necessary to physical well-being. We have to be intentional about engaging in the types of activity our bodies need, including periods of appropriate cardiovascular exertion, exercise aimed at maintaining strength and developing core strength, routines for maintaining balance, and stretching.

Start with ten minutes. Go for a walk. Get in a pool and move around and swim. Today would be a great day to get started.

Hygiene is emphasized in the Bible as well. Sections of Leviticus,

Deutcronomy, and Numbers describe laws that help us avoid infection. God required that the Israelites avoid touching dead bodies, keep corpses away from where people lived, properly dispose of solid waste, and wash their hands, utensils, and clothing in running water instead of stagnant water. Beyond this, God expected his people to follow his guidelines for sexual conduct, pay attention to warnings against consuming animal blood, and avoid contact with the solid waste of animals and humans. These guidelines make perfect sense in light of what we now know about infectious disease.

The importance of sound sleep and adequate rest will be covered in the next chapter. This is a major emphasis in Scripture, and the benefits are profound.

My friends Brian and his parents, Silvio and Katie, have recently come through a very difficult chapter of their lives. Three years ago, when Brian was sixteen, progressively worsening pain in his leg eventually led to a diagnosis of a rare lymphoma that had already spread throughout his bones. Brian's experience reveals the complex anatomy of serious illness.

The previous year his father, Sil, was diagnosed with chronic leukemia and Parkinson's disease, which left Brian feeling abandoned by God. In his words, he was "not on the short list of those he loves," raising the question of whether or not "God had [his] best interest in mind." Brian explained that "my heart and mind were already closed off to the reality of God's love for me, and I did a really good job at hiding it from my friends and family."

His illness proved the very thing that pushed him back into God's arms. He realized his lack of control over life and the lack of wisdom in depending on himself. "I made a decision one day that rather than blame God for my darkness, I would put my trust in him."

The course of treatment was long and difficult, involving not only chemotherapy, but an episode of infection and sepsis which nearly took his life, and complications of treatment, including personality changes, periods of depression, hallucinations, and volatile behavior with days of profanity-laced tirades.

"I think one of the hardest things during this time of mental instability was that though I consciously knew that I was acting out of character, I couldn't stop myself. I remember at times I would cry while I was acting out, but I still couldn't stop myself. I had to lean on God to show me the way because I was so confused as to why it was happening. It was by far the most powerless, helpless feeling I have ever experienced in my life." All of this was confounded by the hurt and confusion he saw in his parents in response to some of his behavior.

Brian is now cancer-free and has regular checkups, but his life has changed. Brian will tell you that he now has a no-matter-what dependence on Jesus that I see evidenced in his life. "I really think that I could not have made it through without God's care and support. I know a lot of people go through these things without believing in God, but I am so grateful that he was there."

Routine maintenance of health is one thing, but more serious health issues pose a different kind of challenge. When faced with serious illness like cancer, we need to understand who we are as people created in God's image to make certain we are addressing every aspect of the illness. As one of my friends put it when his wife was diagnosed with cancer: "Cancer is a beast and it was our intention to throw everything at it that God made available—medication, radiation, good nutrition, prayer, hope, laughter, and anything else we could think of."

Wellness. Wholeness. The Bible explains the nature of our humanity more fully than the way it is defined within our culture. To be truly healthy involves not only the gym but the church, not just knowledge but wisdom, not only organic food but truth, not just medication but hope, not only facts but prayer, not just exercise but godly choices, not only effort, but rest, not just therapy but grace.

seven

SLEEP AND SABBATH REST

Remember the Sabbath day by keeping it holy.
(Exodus 20:8)

Rhythm

A rhythm of rest is woven into the fabric of creation. The average heart beats about 100,000 times per day, 3 billion times in an average lifetime. Part of each heartbeat, driven by electrical activity, is the work of contracting the thick cardiac muscle of the ventricles, the phase called systole. But there is also a rhythmically occurring period of relaxation, dilatation, and filling of these heart chambers known as diastole. Each beat involves work and rest.

The sunset, seasons, dormancy before new growth, sleep, and hibernation are all expressions of the rhythm of nature and creation's need to rest. This rhythm is primordial, written in our spirits, recorded in our DNA.

There is a time for everything,
and a season for every activity under the heavens:

a time to be born and a time to die,
a time to plant and a time to uproot,
a time to kill and a time to heal,
a time to tear down and a time to build,
a time to weep and a time to laugh,
a time to mourn and a time to dance,
a time to scatter stones and a time to gather them,
a time to embrace and a time to refrain from embracing,
a time to search and a time to give up,
a time to keep and a time to throw away,
a time to tear and a time to mend,
a time to be silent and a time to speak,
a time to love and a time to hate,
a time for war and a time for peace. (Ecclesiastes 3:1–8)

But this rhythm can be buried in our busyness, lost like other instincts, drummed out of us by hyper-stimulation and preoccupation. The quiet recognition of it, the ability to sense our need for rest, is part of wholeness.

Sleep

There is a kind of rest we need *every day*. Circadian rhythm is a twenty-four hour cycle, a physiological, neurological, and behavioral process observed in plants, animals, fungi, and even some bacteria. Part of this cycle involves taking cues from the environment about our need for sleep.

My wife loves to go to sleep. And she's very good at it. Unlike me, she can find a way to sleep just about anywhere. Most of the time sleep for me is a necessary interruption of things I'd rather be doing. But I have learned that my waking hours have a higher quality if my sleeping hours are of a sufficient quantity. Sleep is a gift from God.

In peace I will lie down and sleep,
for you alone, O LORD,
make me dwell in safety. (Psalm 4:8)

In vain you rise early
and stay up late,
toiling for food to eat—
for he grants sleep to those he loves. (Psalm 127:2)

It's not completely clear why we need to sleep. It's clear that our brains demand it. Some people have a genetic disorder called FFI, or fatal familial insomnia, a disorder that involves the inability to sleep. Tragically, most people with this disease only live one year after the onset of symptoms. Sleep appears to play a role in memory consolidation, weeding out unnecessary synapses and connections, allowing us to remember what's important.

We need seven and a half to nine hours of sleep each day. The problem of inadequate sleep in the United States is a significant public health issue, as approximately 29 percent of U.S. adults report sleeping less than seven hours per night. In another study involving all fifty states, 70 percent of those surveyed reported at least some days of insufficient rest or sleep in the preceding thirty days.

Sleep deprivation puts us at increased risk for heart disease; type 2 diabetes; mental illness, including psychosis; damage to the brain; increased risk of seizures; a weakened immune system; and a decreased ability to heal wounds. It also leads to loss of productivity, poor concentration, high-risk behaviors, and a lack of ability to function. Sleep deprivation among drivers increases auto accidents to rates comparable to drivers who are legally drunk.

Some of the roadblocks to sound and restful sleep can be addressed by the commonsense principles of sleep hygiene. Stay away from caffeine and other stimulants. Don't nap. Exercise regularly but not right before sleep. Set a sleep schedule. Make sure the bedroom is cool, dark, quiet, and comfortable. Limit fluid intake before sleep. Eat sensibly, and finish your last meal several hours before sleep. Consider a relaxing routine before you go to bed, such as a warm shower or listening to quiet music.

Sabbath

There is also a kind of rest we need *every week*.

The Sabbath is an expression of the intended rhythm of creation. God created, then rested. We are to work six days and rest one (Exodus 31:12–18). Though most Christians worship on Sunday, recognizing Jesus' resurrection on the first day of the week as the center of salvation history, we maintain recognition of a Sabbath rhythm of rest necessary to our well-being. The Sabbath is for expressing Jesus' rule and authority. It is a day for worshiping Jesus and acknowledging by our choices that life is about Jesus and not about our work, accomplishments, and money. When we rest from our labors and our need to make certain things happen, other important things can happen—love, celebration, worship, family, rest—things that are renewing to our whole being.

Jesus never denied the need for Sabbath rest, but he tore the legalism right out of it.

> At that time Jesus went through the grainfields on the Sabbath. His disciples were hungry and began to pick some heads of grain and eat them. When the Pharisees saw this, they said to him, "Look! Your disciples are doing what is unlawful on the Sabbath."
>
> He answered, "Haven't you read what David did when he and his companions were hungry? He entered the house of God, and he and his companions ate the consecrated bread—which was not lawful for them to do, but only for the priests. [At this point in Mark's gospel, we read that Jesus also said, "The Sabbath was made for man, not man for the Sabbath" (Mark 2:27).] Or haven't you read in the Law that the priests on Sabbath duty in the temple desecrate the day and yet are innocent? I tell you that something greater than the temple is here. If you had known what these words mean, "I desire mercy, not sacrifice," you would not have condemned the innocent. For the Son of Man is Lord of the Sabbath.
>
> Going on from that place, he went into their synagogue, and a man with a shriveled hand was there. Looking for a reason to accuse Jesus, they asked him, "Is it lawful to heal on the Sabbath?"
>
> He said to them, "If any of you has a sheep and it falls into a pit

on the Sabbath, will you not take hold of it and lift it out? How much more valuable is a person than a sheep! Therefore it is lawful to do good on the Sabbath."

Then he said to the man, "Stretch out your hand." So he stretched it out and it was completely restored, just as sound as the other. But the Pharisees went out and plotted how they might kill Jesus. (Matthew 12:1–14)

The Sabbath is not about rules. It is not about making a good impression. It is about how human beings were made and our need for restorative rest. The needs of David's men and the requirements of the temple service took precedence over Sabbath rules. In essence, Jesus was saying, *I am in charge of the Sabbath. I made it. It's mine.* The intentions of the law are merciful and loving and sometimes the demands of love take precedence over the commands of ceremonial law. It is designed for rest, relief, and renewal, not to be another burden.

On another occasion Jesus healed a man on the Sabbath and told him to "Get up! Pick up your mat and walk." The Jewish leaders were angry because carrying a mat was work, forbidden on the Sabbath (John 5:1–15). Jesus explained that *"My Father is always at his work to this very day, and I too am working."* The Jewish leaders were furious and wanted to kill him, not only for breaking the Sabbath but also for blasphemy for calling God his father. Jesus told them that he could only do what he saw his Father doing, because "the Father loves the Son and shows him all he does. Yes, and he will show him even greater works than these, so that you will be amazed. For just as the Father raises the dead and gives them life, even so the Son gives life to whom he is pleased to give it" (John 5:16–21).

What is this work that Jesus refers to? When sin comes into the picture through Adam and Eve's disobedience, God ends his Sabbath rest after creation and resumes work. The work is not creation but re-creation necessitated by sin. It is the renewal of all things—a new world and a renewed humanity anticipating a new Sabbath made possible by what Christ accomplishes for us in his death and resurrection. We cannot negate the effects of sin by our work and efforts. We must come to a place where we rest in Jesus, and in what he has accomplished. He is our rest.

> There remains, then, a Sabbath-rest for the people of God; for anyone who enters God's rest also rests from their works, just as God did from his. (Hebrews 4:9–10)

Retreat

There is a kind of rest we need *every so often*.

Jesus often withdrew just to be quiet and rest. When pressed in upon and drained, when confronted with important decisions, when faced with impending death, he got alone with his Father in a quiet place. He sometimes sent crowds away, withdrawing without announcement, seeking solitude when he needed it:

> After he had dismissed them, he went up on a mountainside by himself to pray. Later that night, he was there alone. (Matthew 14:23)

> Very early in the morning, while it was still dark, Jesus got up, left the house and went off to a solitary place, where he prayed. (Mark 1:35)

> Yet the news about him spread all the more, so that crowds of people came to hear him and to be healed of their sicknesses. But Jesus often withdrew to lonely places and prayed. (Luke 5:15–16)

God provided the Israelites with days of remembering his saving acts and the attributes that distinguished him from pagan deities worshiped by their neighbors, celebrations that would preserve for future generations these great events in their history as a people—Purim (Feast of Lots), Passover (Feast of Unleavened Bread), Shavuot (Feast of Weeks), Rosh Hashanah (Jewish New Year), Yom Kippur (Day of Atonement), Sukkot

(Feast of Tabernacles), Shemini Atzeret (Assembly of the Eighth Day), as well as the sabbatical year every seventh year and the year of Jubilee every fiftieth year. These celebrations were described by Moses as "the LORD's appointed festivals, which you are to proclaim as sacred assemblies . . ." involving remembering, celebrating, and offerings, which are "in addition to those for the LORD's Sabbaths . . ." (Leviticus 23:37–38).

Vacations, holidays, retreats, periods of silence and solitude are one more important piece of the rhythm of rest.

Pace

In addition to the rhythm of work and rest is the matter of pace. Many of us need to slow down, reversing our RPMs. We are moving through this world too quickly, missing out on so much that is best in life. Our lives are full, packed like an overstuffed suitcase, leaving no room for some of the most important things necessary to the trip. Without sufficient margins we can be overwhelmed by the next thing demanding our attention. Peace and joy are lost and replaced by impatience. Sometimes more is less: "Better one handful with tranquillity than two handfuls with toil and chasing after the wind" (Ecclesiastes 4:6).

The way I choose to live at times is poor commentary on my view of God. Some of the things I perceive as strengths are the enemy of my relationships and my well-being when not corrected by grace. Left to myself, I am organized, task-oriented, driven, ready for another project, and always in a hurry. What am I trying to prove by the way I push? Whose approval am I trying to gain? Am I purposefully responding to grace or merely driven by a sense of inadequacy and the need to prove myself?

Ernest Becker described the most basic human motivation in terms of the competitive interaction of children. "The child cannot allow himself to be second best or devalued, much less left out. . . . Sibling rivalry is a critical problem that reflects the basic human condition . . . they so openly express man's tragic destiny: he must desperately justify himself as an object of primary value in the universe." This describes so much of my life.

Blaise Pascal explained in his book *Pensees* that "the sole cause of man's unhappiness is that he does not know how to stay quietly in his room." This is true because "what people want is not the easy peaceful life that allows us to think of our unhappy condition . . . but the agitation that takes our mind off it and diverts us."

Pascal also maintained that people "have another secret instinct, left over from the greatness of our original nature, telling them that the only true happiness lies in rest and not in excitement." Excitement and diversion can be confused with rest.

> All our life passes in this way: we seek rest by struggling against certain obstacles, and once they are overcome, rest proves intolerable because of the boredom it produces. We must get away from it and crave excitement.

If we keep busy enough, we can avoid thinking about some of the unpleasantness lurking beneath the surface. But the problems within bubble up and bleed through into our speech and actions and eventually affect our lives at every level.

If we remove the sedating effects of our self-absorption and self-indulgence through stillness, quiet, prayer, fasting, and other spiritual disciplines, we will experience the symptoms of our dysfunctional appetites more fully. Frustration, impulsivity, worry, anxiety, fear, and most certainly anger, will all rise to the surface, revealing the true condition our heart had been in all along. Such insight into our inner selves can certainly be shocking. But it is only when we strip away the props and defenses long enough to face the darkness within that the possibility of new life can emerge.

When we let God prove his love for us in the places where our hearts are messiest, his healing and transformation will come. We will discover that buried beneath our sin, addictions, and self-absorption lies our true hunger—our hunger for God. The alternative to solitude is living the rest of our lives as one long defense against the reality of our condition.

Stress vs. Trust

The stress response, which is set off by several parts of the brain, is a part of life. It helps us rise to challenges and respond quickly. It contributes to feelings of motivation and even happiness. But prolonged stress from the cumulative effect of pressures, demands, and busyness adversely impacts health. It can lead to a rapid heartbeat, headaches, muscle tightness, back pain, gastrointestinal problems, high blood pressure, an increased risk of heart disease, stroke, metabolic syndrome, a diminished immune response, skin problems, depression, anxiety, weight gain, and psychosomatic illnesses. In fact, 60 to 90 percent of doctor visits are for problems related to stress.

Stress affects our thoughts and emotions by making us feel cranky, impatient, and unable to cope with problems. When we're stressed out, we are often unable to focus and have a sense of worry or apprehension over small things.

While stress contributes to health problems, relaxation facilitates healing. Herbert Benson's bestselling book *The Relaxation Response* suggests the need for exercises causing us to relax, a response with proven benefits for health.

I would go a step further and suggest that at another level developing a deep sense of trust will erase fear and stress more thoroughly, allowing us to live in this state of relaxation so that normal stress responses are the interruptions to our baseline.

We are born knowing how to relax. Infants remind us of this as they fall asleep while nursing or doze off in response to repetitive sounds or car rides. But with time we forget, and we come to depend on alternatives to relaxation—medication, soothing addictions, and levels of activity that drown out the call of body and spirit to slow down. But we can learn again to relax.

The source of stress is something deeper than our level of busyness. In fact, our busyness may only be a symptom rather than the cause of our stress. The real issue is that we feel helpless, powerless, and unable to solve life's basic problems. And then we get hit with big problems. We live in a world where everything keeps changing—our relationships, our health and finances, our children, politics. We are faced with constant adjustments.

Yesterday I talked with a friend who told me that her eyelid has been twitching. She has lost two close family members in the last three years, and now her husband is severely ill. She has an eleven-year-old son. She works full-time and is trying to finish a college degree online. She said through her tears, "You have all these ideas about the future, what it will be like. Then things keep happening to take that away from you." That's the essence of our condition. We have less control over things than we realize, and we do everything we can to make things happen the way we think they are supposed to.

The only answer to this comes in understanding that God is up to the job of our trust, that his intentions toward us are entirely good, that he is powerful and competent and able to work things out for good. We need to trust him that the story will end well and that everything will be okay.

This is the kind of rest we need *every minute of every day*. It's what God describes as being still enough to know that he is God (Psalm 46:10), and it involves letting go of the need to control things and to make our own plans work. As one writer put it, you can change the hands of a clock but it doesn't change what time it is. You can open a rosebud before its time, but by doing so you destroy the rose. Cease striving. Hands off. Let go of your need to control things. Jesus constantly invited people to such rest.

Come to me, all you who are weary and burdened, and I will give you rest. (Matthew 11:28)

Look at the birds of the air; they do not sow or reap or store away in barns, and yet your heavenly Father feeds them. Are you not much more valuable than they? Can any one of you by worrying add a single hour to your life? (Matthew 6:26–27)

There is one place where our drive toward busyness can become so saturated by grace that it gives way to a pervasive sense of trust and rest. At the cross we discover that we have nothing to prove to anyone, that only God's opinion of us matters. Our identity is shaped and determined by what Jesus has done, and God's verdict on our lives at the end of time, announced today, is that we are okay; we can actually stand before the God of the universe and hear him say, "I commend you, I accept you, I am pleased with you." There we discover that our lack of control doesn't really matter because the one who is in control loves us. This is where we find rest.

On the hard copy of this chapter are the scrawlings of my three-year-old daughter, Ciara. When I thought I should have been working last night, we spent some time working on writing her name. It was time wasted by my usual standards but the high point of my day. Even as I stare down at her doodles, the leaden feeling in my heart—the product of years of practice at feeling stressed—seeps away, displaced by the memory of mutual giggling and silliness, her hard work and determination, her exultation in small successes, and her ability to unearth the joy in the simplest things.

The last few years I have made a practice of finding ways to not be in a hurry. I am intentionally moving at a slower pace, sometimes getting a little less done, but probably accomplishing more that matters. Once in a while I get to wait in a long line at the market or the bank, and when it happens that I receive an apology for the wait, I love to honestly say, "It's okay. I'm in no hurry."

I have also learned with time that when faced with crisis we need solitude and rest. When I was in high school, I reached a point of crisis. A series of losses, including my broken relationship with my father, had left me pained and discouraged. It was a very dark time for me. I worked in the garden department at K-Mart in the afternoon and on Saturdays. On my way home and sometimes on lunch break I would sneak off to Immaculate Conception, the Catholic church right behind the store. This large church with high ceilings was always open and always cool and quiet. I would just sit there in silence. Sometimes for an hour or two. Until the sun set. I was there with God, quiet, listening. I cannot possibly describe the hope and healing God poured into my soul during those idle hours.

I find that the rumblings beneath the surface—the deepest currents of the spirit, easily ignored but powerful in the way they shape us—can only be sensed in stillness. And in the quiet we discover our real powerlessness and sense of helplessness, our inability to change anything. This sense of need that bubbles to the surface becomes our purest, deepest cry to God. A cry for help. We cannot make God do what we want. We can only wait. But in the waiting, in the silence, in the stillness, we find the One who is able to take care of us, and our hearts relax in the presence of unqualified love.

The powerful healing effects of being alone in a quiet environment have been carefully studied and described—improved self-control, including gaining and losing weight, decreased alcohol consumption, smoking cessation, overcoming fears.

In his book *Ruthless Trust,* Brennan Manning tells the story of John Kavanaugh, an ethicist searching for clarity about what to do with his life. As part of his search, he volunteered to work for three months at the Home for the Dying in Calcutta, India, a ministry founded by Mother Teresa. On his first morning he met Mother Teresa. She asked him, "What can I do for you?" He asked that she pray for him. "What do you want me to pray for?" she asked. He replied, "Pray that I have clarity." Her curt response took him by surprise. "No, I will not do that." When he asked why not, she told him, "Clarity is the last thing you are clinging to and must let go of." When Kavanaugh observed that she seemed to have the kind of clarity he wanted, she laughed and told him, "I have never had clarity; what I have always had is trust. So I will pray that you trust God."

What we want is the information that will keep us safe and in control. What we need is to learn to trust.

Presence

We easily forget that life is a grace we receive one moment at a time. Paul said we are to forget what lies behind, and Jesus warned us not to worry about tomorrow. We are left with the present moment. The moment that just passed is gone forever. The moment to come may never be ours. God invites us to live for him fully in the present moment, recognizing that the kingdom of God is here and now.

Hurry is the enemy of relationship. We cannot fully engage in conversation when we are anticipating what comes next. Many things clamor for our attention at any given moment, but few are as essential to our happiness as relationship and meaningful connection. Relationships require time—to open our hearts, explore the world together in conversation, wonder over the mysteries of life, and do the difficult but joyous work of loving and caring.

I remember a day on which I was quite full of myself. I rushed home from the church to grab a few things I had forgotten, calling out a series of "important" facts to my wife on my way out the door. All this time, Jonathan, eighteen months old, was standing with his hands in the air reaching out for me. I was not paying attention. Carole interrupted my sense of urgency by saying, "Your son would like your attention." I was awakened, stunned by my blindness. Hurry kills love by filling us up with the importance of our own agenda.

These dynamics are especially true in our relationship with God. If I cannot love my son whom I can see, what hope is there for me when it comes to deeply loving God? (1 John 4:20). Busyness robs me of my ability to know God the way he wants to be known. The practices known as the spiritual disciplines are essentially a way of creating time and space in our lives to be with God, to allow him to speak to us, to act in our hearts to reveal and convict and transform.

> In the morning, LORD, you hear my voice;
> in the morning I lay my requests before you
> and wait expectantly. (Psalm 5:3)

Music, play, laughter, and celebration are gifts that are rarely opened by those in a hurry. Like children who never bother opening some of the gifts under the tree, we hurry on to the next thing. Whole chapters of our lives tear past us with little note of how much has happened, how much has changed.

When we slow down, we regain our ability to see, to experience, and to enjoy. Attentiveness restores connection with our environment. Familiarity is a way of seeing without seeing, a skill necessary for those traveling too fast, but a terrible form of blindness. Unlearning familiarity can allow us to regain a sense of awe, to see with the eyes of a child. It moves us from a world that has become monotonous and drab to a world that is vibrant and pulsing.

In his book *He That Is Spiritual*, Lewis Sperry Chafer warns against brands of spirituality that overemphasize negatives, leading us to believe that spirituality is a big drag.

> How misleading is the theory that to be spiritual one must abandon play, diversion, and helpful amusement. . . . Spirituality is not a pious pose. It is not a "Thou shall *not*": it is "Thou *shalt*." It flings open the doors into the eternal blessedness, energies, and resources of God. It is a serious thing to remove the element of relaxation and play from any life. We cannot be normal physically, mentally, or spiritually if we neglect this vital factor in human life. God has provided that our joy shall be full.

Reading between the lines of the Gospels, it is clear that Jesus knew how to frame a story, how to tell a joke well. He knew how to laugh hard and play long. G. K. Chesterton ends his amazing book *Orthodoxy* by describing this aspect of Jesus' character:

> Joy, which was the small publicity of the pagan, is the gigantic secret of the Christian. . . . The tremendous figure that fills the Gospel, towers in this respect, as in every other, above all the thinkers who ever thought themselves tall. His pathos was natural, almost casual. The Stoics, ancient and modern, were proud of concealing their tears. He never concealed His tears; He showed them plainly on His open face at any daily sight, such as the far sight of His native city. Yet He concealed something. Solemn supermen and imperial diplomatists are proud of restraining their anger. He never restrained His anger. He flung furniture down the front steps of the Temple, and asked men how they expected to escape the damnation of Hell. Yet He restrained something. . . . There was something that He hid from all men when He went up a mountain to pray. There was something that He covered constantly by abrupt silence or impetuous isolation. There was some one thing that was too great for God to show us when He walked upon our earth; and I have sometimes fancied that it was His mirth.

Sometimes I go for walks with my three-year-old, Ciara. We walk about halfway down the block on one side of the quiet street where we live, then back toward home down the other side. Her condition makes it difficult to walk. She falls down a lot unless I am holding her hand. She often resists my assistance. Her whole approach to life is a parable in God's pace. When she does fall, she gets right back up without dusting herself off and continues what she was doing, as if to say that life is too full of wonder to waste time on decorum.

Everything she experiences evokes awe. She stands in the shadows of the trees noting the outline. She recognizes her own shadow and the way it follows her movement, and in response she lifts her hands in excited celebration of this incredible miracle. Every bug and puddle, sprinkler-head and flower must be explored. One foot of earth is filled with more awe for her than all of Europe for many. Last week we saw a bird that had built her nest in a bush off our front porch, feeding her two little ones. Ciara stood particularly tall, rocked up on her toes over and over, clapping her hands at this sight that overwhelmed her, as if she could not tolerate the joy or absorb the goodness.

She reminds me that my most ordinary days are filled with miracles—the deep green of the olive tree, the explosive purple of the jacarandas, the delicate scent of orange blossoms, the dancing sound of a woman speaking Mandarin into her cell phone, the squealing laughter of children at play, the relieving effect of a quiet word of encouragement, a belly laugh over a well-told joke.

PART 4:

Insight for Our Relationship With Creation

eight

STEWARDSHIP

For six years sow your fields, and for six years prune your
vineyards and gather their crops. But in the seventh year the
land is to have a year of sabbath rest,
a sabbath to the LORD.
(LEVITICUS 25:3–4)

Joy

Creation is an act of love. The variety of sound, color, texture, temperature, scent, taste, climate, species, its complexity and vastness, coupled with our capacity for joy and pleasure, our aesthetic sense, our eagerness for learning and exploration, our physical senses with which we engage all that God has made, provide an exquisite picture of a Creator playfully and lovingly engaged in crafting an environment that reflects his goodness for creatures he loved long before he made them. An ocean breeze wafting over us cool and sweet. An image from the Hubble telescope of massive pillars of gas from a star-forming region of a nebula with unimaginable depth and brilliance. A moment of wonder over the expansiveness of the universe. Each is an expression of grace.

We break the skin of an orange, the color and scent drawing us in. As micro-vesicles burst, producing a fine mist, we experience a tiny spray of coolness, which inhaled dances across olfactory buds, producing a chemical-electronic cascade shooting through our brain across millions of neurons, producing a sensation of fragrance that tickles our spirit, causing an all but imperceptible sensation of joy—an easily ignored sense that there is someone there who made all this for us and designed us to experience it. We are loved.

The heavens declare the glory of God (Psalm 19:1), the truth about his character is written across the face of creation (Romans 1:19–20), and we sense at moments that what he made is, as he called it, "very good" (Genesis 1:31).

In 1970, Francis Schaeffer wrote his outstanding book *Pollution and the Death of Man: The Christian View of Ecology* in response to two articles. One expressed the opinion that the Christian worldview places man in dominion over nature, thus providing the basis for human abuse of nature; the other argued that the solution to this problem is found in pantheism and learning to view humankind and the rest of nature as a singular essence. While Schaeffer exposes the inadequacy of pantheism as a worldview, he also expresses concern about the view of nature reflected in the attitudes of Christians. He wrote,

> Near the end of his life, Darwin acknowledged several times in his writings that two things had become dull to him as he got older. The first was his joy in the arts and the second his joy in nature. This is very intriguing. Darwin offered his proposition that nature, including man, is based only on the impersonal plus time plus chance, and he had to acknowledge at the end of his life that it had had these adverse effects on him. I believe that what we are seeing today is the same loss of joy in our total culture as Darwin personally experienced. . . . The distressing thing about this is that orthodox Christians often have no

better sense about these things than unbelievers. The death of "joy" in nature is leading to the death of nature itself.

Later Schaeffer describes his experience of lecturing at a Christian school in the 1960s. Across the ravine from the school was a "hippie community" that practiced pagan rituals and utilized pagan symbols and ideas. While visiting the commune, he was struck by the beauty of the community and their care of the land. The leader of the commune actually commented on the "ugliness" of the Christian school.

> It was then that I realized what a horrible situation this was. When I stood on the Christian ground and looked at the Bohemian people's place, it was beautiful. They had even gone to the trouble of running their electric cables under the level of the trees so that they couldn't be seen. Then I stood on the pagan ground and looked at the Christian community and saw ugliness. That is horrible. Here you have a Christianity that is failing to take into account man's responsibility and proper relationship to nature.

The question suggested here is important to our well-being: What view are we to take of nature? What value are we to place on it? What is our relationship to it?

Toward a Biblical View of Nature

Most of the attitudes toward nature within our culture can be summarized in a few broad concepts.

Pantheism is the belief that what is ultimate or divine in the universe is the material world, the universe as a singular essence. It is the deification or worship of nature. It places a high value on nature as a unified whole, but the particulars have no real meaning. Any sense of human specialness is lost, along with the categories by which we understand our relationship to the rest of creation. In other words, we are no different than a tree or a parakeet or even a golf ball.

Many popular books promote this worldview, romanticizing nature and at times encouraging regret over our loss of a more primitive way of life. The media has provided a sanitized and carefully crafted view of nature.

Anyone who has explored nature beyond the confines of their own backyard is aware that it does not share our sensibilities and morals. It seems to be guided in many places by the harsh law of the "survival of the fittest." In fact, one of the more popular arguments against the existence of the Judeo-Christian God has to do with the destructive force of nature—events like tsunamis and earthquakes. If there is an all-good, all-powerful God, how could he allow such things to happen? As one writer put it, the world "is filled with pathogens, parasites, and predators that give life on Earth such a bloody and painful character."

> Earth contains earthquakes, volcanoes, and floods as well as bacteria and viruses that kill innocent children, not to mention sinful adults. Many kinds of pagan Gods, especially ones that permit or cause cruelty and pain, are much more compatible with the reality of life on Earth than the Christian God. . . . The only inescapable conclusion from the problem of evil is that the all-loving, all-powerful Christian God is a human fantasy—a projection of our fondest emotions and desires.

Sam Harris's entire argument against a benevolent God rests on two assertions—that God should prevent all natural disasters such as hurricanes, and that God is to blame for all human-caused disasters such as genocides. "Atheism is nothing more than the noises reasonable people make . . . given the relentless destruction of innocent human beings we witness in the world each day."

Ironically, the ten most devastating nature-driven disasters in recorded history have claimed less than 10 percent of the lives lost in one human-nature-driven disaster—World War II. Humans remain their own worst enemy. Nevertheless, nature remains a source of suffering and death, and the closer we get to it the more we are aware of this fact.

The pursuit of an answer to the problem of evil, specifically the problem of evil within nature, has no answer in pantheism except to label whatever nature dishes up as "normal" and "natural." The Christian, on the other hand, can answer the problem of evil in nature and stand in defiant opposition to it. The lack of benevolence, the evil within nature, is caused by the reverberating effects of sin as it rolls through the universe. The Christian view of God's character and the "disorder" within nature is described by Charles Spurgeon in his comments on Psalm 145:

> Kindness is the law of the universe. . . . The Creator is never rough, the Provider is never forgetful, the Ruler is never cruel. Nothing is done to create disease, no organs are arranged to promote misery; the incoming of sickness and pain is not according to original design, but a result of our disordered state. Man's body as it left the Maker's hand was neither framed for disease, decay, nor death, neither was the purpose of it discomfort and anguish; far otherwise, it was framed for a joyful activity, and a peaceful enjoyment of God.

It is difficult to grasp the extent of sin's effects. If sin harms us physically, emotionally, and spiritually, isn't it possible that it affects us genetically, ecologically, and in other ways? There is much we can do to stand in opposition to these effects—we "fight" to live, we "fight" disease, we "fight" to save lives. We are compelled to do this because we understand that things are not as they were intended to be, things have purpose and meaning, not all things are the same, and human beings are not merely one more species. The instinct to resist evil makes no sense if a human being is no more valuable than an ant, if there are no distinctions and categories within creation.

The same lack of categories found in pantheism occurs in other areas of philosophy. Peter Singer, writing as an ethicist, finds no real difference between a human and a pig when he applies a pragmatic approach to the value of life. In fact, a normal pig has more rights than an infirmed child by Singer's standards, based on a perceived level of consciousness and awareness. Without categories, without some way of defining and describing our value and our relationship to the rest of creation, everyone loses.

One columnist points out that pantheism provides "a form of religion that even atheists can support."

Richard Dawkins has called pantheism "a sexed-up atheism." (He means that as a compliment.) Sam Harris concluded his polemic "The End of Faith" by rhapsodizing about the mystical experiences available from immersion in "the roiling mystery of the world." Citing Albert Einstein's expression of religious awe at the "beauty and sublimity" of the universe, Dawkins allows, "In this sense I too am religious."

In fact, pantheism demonstrates the essence of sin, evil, rebellion, and independence from God, as those who embrace it choose what Paul describes as the worship of the natural world rather than the One who created it.

For although they knew God, they neither glorified him as God nor gave thanks to him, but their thinking became futile and their foolish hearts were darkened. Although they claimed to be wise, they became fools and exchanged the glory of the immortal God for images made to look like a mortal human being and birds and animals and reptiles.

Therefore God gave them over in the sinful desires of their hearts to sexual impurity for the degrading of their bodies with one another. They exchanged the truth of God for a lie, and worshiped and served created things rather than the Creator—who is forever praised. Amen. (Romans 1:21–25)

A second attitude toward nature is expressed in some forms of the concept of *dualism*, which minimize the significance of the material world. This view tends to divorce us from our context as creatures within creation, reducing what really matters to the immaterial world—our soul, salvation, life beyond death, heaven. Platonic dualism claims that the natural world, which is constantly changing, is an imperfect reflection of the permanent and heavenly world of ideas or forms. Plato described the person as an immortal soul imprisoned in a mortal body. This type of dualism, which contributed to heresies in the early church, such as Gnosticism and Docetism, tends to emphasize that the spiritual is higher and the physical is lower.

The early church rejected such dualism by emphasizing the incarnation, the resurrection, and the coming redemption of all of creation (1 Corinthians 15:22–25; Romans 8:19–21). Jesus, the eternal Word, assumes our humanity in the incarnation. Both the Hebrew Scriptures and the New Testament anticipate the coming redemption of all of creation at the end of time. Even in 2 Corinthians 4 and 5, where Paul contrasts the seen and the unseen, and the temporary and the eternal—which might be used to make a case for dualism—he points to the *bodily* resurrection of Jesus. This resurrection is the reason for our hope, anticipating the bodily resurrection of the dead at the end of time and the new creation and the reconciliation of the world to God. Physical things may be "low" in relationship to other things, but they are not low simply because they are physical. In fact, the biblical emphasis on the physical resurrection and the renewal of creation gives greater meaning and importance to life here and now, allowing Paul to claim that what we do for Jesus now makes a difference that will matter forever (1 Corinthians 15:7–10).

While pantheism has too high a view of nature, some forms of dualism tend to dismiss its significance and make it low and unimportant. In contrast to these two philosophical views, Francis Schaeffer points us to a *biblical view* of creation.

In his book *Pollution and the Death of Man*, he begins with the realization that we are all created, made from nothing, by an infinite God. We share with the rest of creation that we are creatures, finite and dependent. We have a clear relationship with everything created.

At the same time, this infinite God is personal. He chooses to create humans in his image and makes us unique in creation. Schaeffer wrote, "Christians reject the view that there is no distinction . . . between man and other things; and they reject the view that man is totally separate from all other things."

In other words, we are a part of creation but special among creation. The psalmist wrote:

> When I consider your heavens,
> the work of your fingers,
> the moon and the stars,
> which you have set in place,
> what is mankind that you are mindful of them,
> human beings that you care for them?
> You have made them a little lower than the angels
> and crowned them with glory and honor.
> You made them rulers over the works of your hands;
> you put everything under their feet:
> all flocks and herds,
> and the animals of the wild,
> the birds in the sky,
> and the fish in the sea,
> all that swim the paths of the seas.
> O LORD, our Lord,
> how majestic is your name in all the earth! (Psalm 8:3–9)

This view taken seriously produces a *humility* that grows out of our awareness of having been created, but at the same time provides a *specialness* because of the dignity that God gives us. Our relationship to creation, even toward a tree cut down for firewood, is characterized by respect because that tree was made by God. But we do not romanticize or idealize it or treat it as having the same value as a person. Instead, we live as people who have "a reason for dealing with each created thing on a high level of respect."

Isaiah wrote:

> Lift up your eyes and look to the heavens:
> Who created all these?
> He who brings out the starry host one by one
> and calls forth each of them by name.

> Because of his great power and mighty strength,
> not one of them is missing. (Isaiah 40:26)

In the observable universe there are actually a trillion (1,000,000,000,000) stars in each of a trillion galaxies, totaling 1 x 10^{24} (1,000,000,000,000,000,000,000,000) stars. God is aware of each one of them and each has meaning to him.

Jesus constantly delighted in creation, pointing to the wisdom of birds and flowers and crops in teaching us how to live. He said we are worth much more than a sparrow. But notice he did not say that the sparrow is worthless. In fact, it has God's attention (Matthew 10:29–31). In reference to the Sabbath, he said, "If any of you has a sheep and it falls into a pit on the Sabbath, will you not take hold of it and lift it out? How much more valuable is a person than a sheep! Therefore it is lawful to do good on the Sabbath" (Matthew 12:11–12). He places value on the sheep while again asserting transcendent human value.

As Jonah grieves over God's acceptance of Nineveh's repentance and his refusal to destroy Nineveh, God says to Jonah: "Should I not have concern for the great city of Nineveh, in which there are more than a hundred and twenty thousand people who cannot tell their right hand from their left—and also many animals?" (Jonah 4:10–11). God's primary concern is clearly for the people of Nineveh, but his concern for these animals should not be ignored. In the Exodus, the blood of a lamb placed on the doorframes saved not only the Hebrews but also their animals (Exodus 11–12).

Over and over again, God declares his love and compassion for all the things he created:

> The LORD is good to all;
> he has compassion on all he has made. . . .
> The LORD is trustworthy in all he promises
> and faithful in all he does.
> The LORD upholds all who fall
> and lifts up all who are bowed down.

The eyes of all look to you,
and you give them their food at the proper time.
You open your hand
and satisfy the desires of every living thing. (Psalm 145:9, 13–16)

Commenting on verse 9, Charles Spurgeon wrote, "The duty of kindness to animals may logically be argued from this verse. Should not the children of God be like their Father in kindness?"

Many aspects of the environmental movement stem from ideologies foreign to biblical thought, and Christians tend to see many environmental issues strapped to pagan ideas and worship of the earth. But the Bible does not allow us the option of ignoring our relationship with creation. Pantheism engages people in the worship of creation. Dualism may lead people to ignore creation or treat it as irrelevant. Scripture invites us to find joy in creation, to discover in it expressions of God's character, to see it as a gracious gift entrusted to us by God and therefore worthy of our care and respect.

There are moments in which I am seized by the sheer miracle of it all—delivering a baby and holding a tiny human being in my hands, standing in the shadowy depths of a pristine grove of California redwoods as wisps of sun sneak through—I am overwhelmed by a sense of my smallness and the greatness and glory of the One who made it all.

Stewardship

In God's explanation to Adam and Eve regarding their relationship to creation, he used a series of descriptions to express his intentions:

> . . . rule over the fish of the sea and the birds in the sky, over the livestock and all the wild animals, and over all the creatures that move along the ground. (Genesis 1:26, 28)

> Be fruitful and increase in number; fill the earth and subdue it. (Genesis 1:28)

> I give you every seed-bearing plant on the face of the whole earth and every tree that has fruit with seed in it. They will be yours for food. (Genesis 1:29)

> The LORD God took the man and put him in the Garden of Eden to work it and take care of it. (Genesis 2:15)

After the flood some aspects of his instructions changed:

> God blessed Noah and his sons, saying to them, "Be fruitful and increase in number and fill the earth. . . . Everything that lives and moves about will be food for you. Just as I gave you the green plants, I now give you everything" (Genesis 9:1–3).

Then God makes a covenant with Noah and his family and with all living things:

> Then God said to Noah and to his sons with him: "I now establish my covenant with you and with your descendants after you and with every living creature that was with you—the birds, the livestock and all the wild animals, all those that came out of the ark with you—every living creature on earth. I establish my covenant with you: Never again will all life be cut off by the waters of a flood; never again will there be a flood to destroy the earth."
>
> And God said, "This is the sign of the covenant I am making between me and you and *every living creature with you,* a covenant for all generations to come: I have set my rainbow in the clouds, and it will be the sign of the covenant between me and the earth. Whenever I bring clouds over the earth and the rainbow appears in the clouds, I will remember my covenant between me and you and *all living creatures of every kind.* Never again will the waters become a flood to destroy *all life.* Whenever the rainbow appears in the clouds, I will see it and remember *the everlasting covenant between God and all living creatures of every kind on the earth*" (Genesis 9:8–16).

The picture that emerges from the prologue of the Bible (Genesis 1–11) is one of benevolent stewardship. Humans are to take what is needed for food and provision, but they are to exercise stewardship—not only to subdue and develop creation but also to "take care of it."

Part of our stewardship grows out of an awareness of God's provision for us through what he has made. In Psalm 105, the psalmist praises God because he provides fresh water and "food from the earth" for our health and enjoyment.

Dominion is not ownership. It all belongs to God. "The earth is the LORD's, and everything in it, the world, and all who live in it" (Psalm 24:1). That God gives us dominion indicates that creation is ultimately his dominion. The premise is a very simple one. God basically says, *I designed it. I created it. It belongs to me. I am God. Show some respect.* This is not the basis for some radical political agenda but important truth that should provide guidance in our choices about how to live. If I borrow my friend's house and pool and fail to take care of it, in fact, damaging his property and trashing it, I would expect him to be upset. This world is God's. When we love him, we want to take care of what belongs to him. When we take care of God's handiwork, we show respect for the One who made it.

God's ownership of creation is reflected in the law. All the firstfruits of the ground and of animals and even human beings (Exodus, chapters 13–34) were offered to God in recognition of his ownership.

This benevolent stewardship of creation is also seen in the laws of justice and mercy (Exodus 23:10–11; Leviticus 25:4–7). For six years the Israelites were to sow and harvest their fields, vineyards, and olive groves, but for the seventh year, they were to let the land rest. The poor were allowed to get food from the land during this time, and animals were allowed to eat.

Sabbath rest included not only the Israelites but their animals as well (Exodus 20:10; 23:12; Deuteronomy 5:14). Trees were protected by the law from the ravages of war (Deuteronomy 20:19). Every Jubilee, or fiftieth year, all land was returned to its original owner (Leviticus 25) to remind the children of Israel that the land belongs to God. He reminds them "the land is mine" and they are his guests, aliens passing through (v. 23).

A Ragged and Eager Creation

Paul describes the effects of human sin on creation:

> The creation waits in eager expectation for the children of God
> to be revealed. For the creation was subjected to frustration, not by
> its own choice, but by the will of the one who subjected it, in hope
> that the creation itself will be liberated from its bondage to decay and
> brought into the freedom and glory of the children of God.
> We know that the whole creation has been groaning as in the
> pains of childbirth right up to the present time. Not only so, but we
> ourselves, who have the firstfruits of the Spirit, groan inwardly as we
> wait eagerly for our adoption to sonship, the redemption of our bod-
> ies. (Romans 8:19–23)

A stressed and ragged creation hampered by the effects of human
sin and the misuse of our freedom has been "subjected to frustration"
and is in "bondage to decay." It is eagerly waiting, groaning in pain, and
anticipating its liberation on that final day, when the power of Jesus'
resurrection leads to "the redemption of our bodies" and the restoration
of all things.

As we have already seen, sin not only destroys our relationships with
God, others, and self, but produces endless negative effects on creation.
Immediately after sin entered the world, God pointed to several initial
effects, including the pain of childbirth and the infestation of the soil
with weeds and thorns, making it more difficult to produce crops, leading to "painful toil" and "sweat" (Genesis 3:16–19).

God creates all things good. He is good, and all that he creates is
essentially good. But he also creates personalities with the freedom to
choose. And the misuse of this freedom is the portal through which
evil enters the world. Evil is a by-product of sin and the misuse of our
freedom. And one of the effects of our tendency to ignore what God has
told us is the strain of human disobedience on creation.

The strain of human sin on creation is witnessed by all of us in many ways.

Crops require nutrient-rich soil to grow well. Farming practices that don't allow for the accumulation of important nutrients through land rest or crop rotation cause the soil to become depleted. God commands us to take care of the soil and to preserve its fertility as an acknowledgment that it is all his. Such laws are for our good and the good of creation.

A few years ago, I went to Maine for the wedding of two friends. I visited a camp called Chop Point on a point of land formed by the convergence of rivers in Woolwich, Maine. The location was breathtaking. The director of the camp told me that when they purchased the land it had little value because the water was so polluted by the dumping of local industry. When such dumping was first regulated by law, he was concerned about the impact of these regulations on local businesses. Within twenty years the rivers were clean and clear, and the recovery of the river's health and the impact on fish and wildlife was so remarkable that everyone recognized it as a win.

The San Gabriel Valley, near Los Angeles, where I grew up, was often blanketed on many days from late spring to early fall. Copper-colored smog filled the air, making it impossible to see the foothills just blocks away, and keeping us indoors and unable to play in the school yard. Though particulate pollution remains a problem, after years of controlling vehicle emissions, one never sees a day like that anymore. Concerns like air pollution, water pollution, noise pollution, water use and supply, soil erosion, species loss, deforestation, and fisheries depletion are challenges to the benevolent stewardship of creation, things that cannot simply be ignored.

Again, Scripture establishes a boundary that leads to health for us and for all of creation. There is a strong connection between our relationship with God and our relationship with creation. Human sin led to expulsion from Eden. And human disobedience carries with it continued consequences in our relationship with creation. Sometimes we can see a direct link between our choices and the harm done, but at other times the connection is more surprising. For example, in the laws in Leviticus governing relationships and sexual purity, we find a curious connection between obedience and relationship with the land. God explains that if his people ignore his laws and persist in defiling the land by their sexual immorality, the land itself will "vomit you out" (Leviticus 18:26–28).

The real and ultimate cause of pollution is human sin. The land vomits out the disobedient. Conversely, the people who do what God asks and walk in his ways remain in the land.

> If you really change your ways and your actions and deal with each other justly, if you do not oppress the foreigner, the fatherless or the widow and do not shed innocent blood in this place, and if you do not follow other gods to your own harm, then I will let you live in this place, in the land I gave your ancestors for ever and ever. (Jeremiah 7:5–7)

> This is what the Sovereign LORD says: "Since you eat meat with the blood still in it and look to your idols and shed blood, should you then possess the land? You rely on your sword, you do detestable things, and each of you defiles his neighbor's wife. Should you then possess the land?" Say this to them: This is what the Sovereign LORD says: "As surely as I live, those who are left in the ruins will fall by the sword, those out in the country I will give to the wild animals to be devoured, and those in strongholds and caves will die of a plague. I will make the land a desolate waste, and her proud strength will come to an end, and the mountains of Israel will become desolate so that no one will cross them. Then they will know that I am the LORD, when I have made the land a desolate waste because of all the detestable things they have done" (Ezekiel 33:25–29).

Pollution is much more than the problems of waste and contamination of water and air. Human sin pollutes the earth. Pollution takes place when we do things our way, refuse God's lordship, and see ourselves as the ones in control. When we feel free to do with creation whatever we please, it becomes one more stage on which God's will is not being done.

We are "fearfully and wonderfully made," created in the image of

God. And God trusts his creation to our care. But we are also creatures, finite and dependent. Our role is to relate to creation in a way that glorifies the Creator, acknowledges his lordship and ownership, and extends his kingdom by doing what he asks.

nine

CREATION AND THE GOAL OF HISTORY

The Son is the image of the invisible God, the firstborn over
all creation. For in him all things were created: things in
heaven and on earth, visible and invisible, whether thrones
or powers or rulers or authorities; all things have been created
through him and for him. He is before all things, and in him
all things hold together. And he is the head of the body, the
church; he is the beginning and the firstborn from among the
dead, so that in everything he might have the supremacy. For
God was pleased to have all his fullness dwell in him, and
through him to reconcile to himself all things, whether things
on earth or things in heaven, by making peace through
his blood, shed on the cross.
(COLOSSIANS 1:15–20)

What Will Be

At the end of time as we know it, Paul tells us that through Jesus, God
will "reconcile to himself all things." Notice the emphasis Paul places
on "everything" and "all things." God is in the process of restoring and

healing the whole mess created by sin. Everything that has been broken and ruined will be reconciled, redeemed, and restored. At the end of time Jesus will declare, "I am making everything new!"

We live between two trees. At the beginning of the story we read:

> Now the LORD God had planted a garden in the east, in Eden; and there he put the man he had formed. And the LORD God made all kinds of trees grow out of the ground—trees that were pleasing to the eye and good for food. In the middle of the garden were the *tree of life* and the tree of the knowledge of good and evil. *A river watering the garden flowed from Eden.* (Genesis 2:8–10)

And at the end of the story . . .

> Then the angel showed me *the river of the water of life*, as clear as crystal, flowing from the throne of God and of the Lamb down the middle of the great street of the city. On each side of the river stood the *tree of life*, bearing twelve crops of fruit, yielding its fruit every month. And the leaves of the tree are for the healing of the nations. (Revelation 22:1–2)

What John describes here in Revelation 22 is the restoration of Eden, a time when everything will be made as it should be, as God always intended. Jesus described this moment as "the renewal of all things" (Matthew 19:28), or literally, the "new genesis." The first chapter of the Bible shows how God made the world. The last one shows how he will remake it.

Most scientists now tell us that the universe is coming to an end. It had a beginning and is in a state of continual expansion. In fact, I recently heard one astronomer describe it as "the runaway universe," a universe expanding faster than anyone imagined. The second law of thermodynamics tells us that this process cannot continue forever, but that eventually all the stored energy will be exhausted, equilibrium will be reached, and the energy needed to drive the universe and sustain life will be gone. Physicists now tend to reject the idea that there is enough energy to cause the universe to contract back on itself. A slow burnout seems inevitable.

For some this may deepen a sense of futility. For others it may be one more argument against materialism, pantheism, and the worship of creation, one more piece of evidence for the veracity of Christian hope.

The implications of a finite universe for the sciences are huge. The way in which physics and astronomy have pointed to a beginning point for the universe, in many ways making God necessary to the universe, has caused some scientists to scramble to find a way of seeing the universe that makes God appear irrelevant to its cause once again. One such attempt is described in Stephen Hawking's recent book, *The Grand Design*. I had hopes that reading the book would provide some grist for intellectual challenge and stimulation, but what I found was a great deal of implausibility laced with statements that are provocative at best. In an astonishing statement in the acknowledgments, the writers reflect the kind of pride that the Bible describes as driving human alienation from God: "The universe has a design, and so does a book. But unlike the universe, a book does not appear spontaneously from nothing. A book requires a creator."

God is not dependent upon or bound to creation. Long before there was time and space, he was there, and when this world as we know it is gone, there will still be One who made it all.

> Lift up your eyes to the heavens,
> look at the earth beneath;
> the heavens will vanish like smoke,
> the earth will wear out like a garment
> and its inhabitants die like flies.
> But my salvation will last forever,
> my righteousness will never fail. (Isaiah 51:6)

The promise of a new heaven and earth is sometimes accompanied by descriptions of the destruction of the heavens and the earth (Mark 13:31; 2 Peter 3:10; Revelation 16:17–21; 21:1). But this stripping down or destruction is not for the sake of obliteration but for the sake of healing. The goal is a renewed creation. A doctor debrides a wound by removing the infected, rotting tissue to promote healing by allowing healthy tissue to grow. The problems caused by sin run deep. The restoration of all things requires both the destruction of evil and renewal. The point is not that creation is dispensable and therefore unimportant, but that God goes to great lengths to destroy evil and renew all of creation. Creation matters to God.

God is not restrained by nature or bound by the laws of physics. He is not limited by the inevitable consequences of human sin. The coming restoration of all things is an expression of his transcendence and his intention to bring about what he has always intended for this world. The outcome of the history of this world will not be determined by human optimism or potential, science, technology, genetic engineering, the influence of the state, or any other human effort. It will be shaped by God's will and by the resurrection of Jesus from the dead, which made real God's power to interrupt the seemingly inevitable.

One day we will fully realize Paul's assurance "that in all things God works for the good of those who love him, who have been called according to his purpose" (Romans 8:28). On that day, every setback—the illness of a loved one, the death of a child, physical disability, pain, suffering, and sorrow—will be answered by God. We will discover why Paul described the pains and struggles of this life as "light and momentary" (2 Corinthians 4:17). God will place upon each of us "an eternal glory" that is so astonishing and magnificent that we will look back at this part of our lives in light of eternity and somehow grasp God's purpose in all of it. I am not sure what that "eternal glory" will entail, but I know it means that the last enemy, death, will be destroyed, swallowed up in victory, and cast into the lake of fire. The specific expression of that victory will be our bodily resurrection. "There will be no more death or mourning or crying or pain, for the old order of things has passed away" (Revelation 21:4). It means that we will see Jesus face-to-face, that God himself will wipe every tear from our eyes. We will be restored to the people we have loved who have followed Jesus. We will enter into a life of worship and purpose and joy more wonderful than we can now imagine.

This is more than a happy ending. It is the real beginning, the story God set out to tell—interrupted by human rebellion—the life he always intended. C. S. Lewis, at the end of the seven book series *The Chronicles of Narnia*, describes the circumstances under which Jill and Eustace learn they have died in a train accident. He wrote a paragraph so beautiful and so rich in truth that I consider it one of the best literary bites I have ever consumed:

> The things that began to happen after that were so great and beautiful that I cannot write them. And for us this is the end of all stories, and we can most truly say that they all lived happily ever after. But for them it was only the beginning of the real story. All their life in this world and all their adventures in Narnia had only been the cover and the title page: now at last they were beginning Chapter One of the Great Story which no one on earth has read: which goes on forever and ever: in which every chapter is better than the one before.

Life here and now is not a trifle. The choices we make have eternal repercussions. But this life is only the prelude to the real story about to begin.

Paul describes the culmination of human history as one in which Jesus, who has conquered and eradicated sin, death, and evil, will lay a renewed creation at the feet of his Father (1 Corinthians 15:24–26). We will witness the unity of all things under Jesus' rule (Ephesians 1:10): the church, the people of God, prepared as a bride for her husband, the new Jerusalem, coming down out of heaven to earth; what the hymn writer Maltbie Babcock described:

> This is my Father's world. O let me ne'er forget
> That though the wrong seems oft so strong, God is the ruler yet.
> This is my Father's world: the battle is not done:
> Jesus Who died shall be satisfied,
> And earth and Heav'n be one.

When John hears the voices of heaven after the sounding of the final trumpet, they are crying out: "The kingdom of the world has become the kingdom of our Lord and of his Christ, and he will reign for ever and ever" (see Revelation 11:15). All of creation waits on tiptoe with consuming anticipation for that day, the moment when Jesus will exert the full-blown dimensions, meaning, significance, and power of his resurrection, making all things new.

To understand this fully we need a robust theology of the kingdom of God, an understanding of why this teaching of the coming of the kingdom was central to Jesus' ministry. The kingdom of God is that place where God's will is being done on earth the way it is already done in heaven. Every time Jesus healed the sick, cast out demons, brought the dead to life, fed the hungry, loved a sinner, forgave sins, or proclaimed the gospel, he was engaged in kingdom-building activity. We are set free, rescued by God, in order to become participants with Jesus in the rescue effort already underway. Jesus invites us to partner with him in dragging the future kingdom of God into the present moment through obedient service, prayer, and the proclamation of the gospel.

We are not just redeemed. We are redeemed by God. We are redeemed for God. And we are redeemed with a purpose. We are new creations. The old is gone and the new has come! We have been reconciled to God by Christ and are called to reconcile the world to God as Christ's ambassadors, allowing God to make his appeal to others through us (2 Corinthians 5:17–20). We are God's co-workers (1 Corinthians 3:9).

With every child lovingly served, the needs of widows and orphans addressed, human trafficking opposed, a well dug, a hospital built, the gospel shared, a sermon preached, the enemy's agenda rejected in prayer, a song or poem or work of art produced for God's glory; when we love others as ourselves, when we love as we have been loved, when we forgive as we have been forgiven, every time our words and actions allow others to see how wonderful Jesus is, we participate with him in pushing out the borders of his kingdom. We share in the renewal of all things and contribute to the new creation—a project Jesus intends to soon complete.

Michael was a two-year-old with Down's syndrome, severely retarded, respirator-dependent, and hospitalized with a resistant pneumonia. Except for the quiet blowing of the ventilator, his room was strangely quiet and empty. No one came to visit. His mother was in prison. He had no other family. He lived in a home for respirator-dependent patients. Since Michael never responded to those around him and usually writhed and made crying sounds throughout his waking hours, taking care of him could seem difficult and thankless.

While rotating at a pediatric hospital, I was assigned to his care. I spent whatever free time I had with Michael. On a day when he seemed particularly inconsolable, I stood at his bedside for quite some time, determined just to be with him in his misery, talking gently, alternately stroking the top of his head then his calf. After about forty minutes, though fully awake, he became very relaxed as if content. I was surprised, since he had never responded this way before. I found one of the nurses who cared for him frequently and together we waited to see if he responded the same way a second time. Sure enough, after thirty or forty minutes he relaxed, a level of response that none of the staff had ever experienced. We became teammates along with others in offering him a new level of care and attention. We strung some toys over his crib. We brought in a cassette player and began to play some pleasant music. More time was spent talking to him and soothing him. His second birthday had come and gone without fanfare weeks earlier. Though late, we planned a party and gathered in Michael's room with a cake, sang to him, and verbalized our affection.

I believe that the kingdom of God was brought into that room because a helpless child with no family was being allowed to experience the truth about his life—that he has a Father who loves him more than you and I can possibly understand.

What Can We Do?

If we take the Bible seriously, we are not just called to reconciliation and healing one day in the future. We are to participate now. Francis Schaeffer wrote: "A Christian-based science and technology should consciously try to see nature substantially healed, while waiting for the future complete healing at Christ's return." How can we allow our lifestyles to be informed by a biblical view of nature? What are some things we can do that might allow us to move in the direction of a "substantial healing"?

First of all, rejoice! Allow God to help you understand what we can know about him through creation. Repeatedly in the Psalms we are told to revel in creation, to praise the Lord who made the seas, the mountains, wild animals, and the stars in the heavens. We can drink in the beauty and the wonder of what he has made and recognize appropriately the value he places on it.

Secondly, we can become stewards of creation as one more avenue for glorifying God. We can participate today in the redemption that God is bringing—leaving each place we visit better because we were there. While on vacation we can clean and repair the park or campsite. My sister in Mexico picks up all the roadside trash for about a half mile in both directions on the highway where she lives. We can adopt a block and offer to help do things that might improve the immediate environment within our neighborhoods.

We can make our homes, churches, schools, and businesses friendly to the environment—reducing waste, creating a recycling system, and planting some trees. Reducing waste is simple and likely familiar to most—refuse (don't buy things you don't need), reuse, recycle.

We need to develop a sense of the consequence of our choices. Try to understand the upstream and downstream effects of what we do. What is the cost of the choice to consume a resource—in water, energy, and in the life of the people who helped produce it? It has been calculated that every pound of beef consumed requires twelve thousand gallons of water compared to sixty gallons for a pound of potatoes. And what will be the unintended consequences of that choice? What will it take to dispose of the refuse and to deal with any other fallout? Or to put it differently, we need to live with an awareness of the impact of our choices—down stream, down wind, next door, and on the other side of the world—and make choices that are thoughtful and loving.

I believe that our treatment of creation is symptomatic of a larger problem—our loss of the sense of life's value, seen in our neglect of children and the least of these. Caring for people is part of caring for creation. How can we hope to be benevolent stewards of creation in a culture that ignores the obvious value of people, those created in God's image? In a world where children are often conceived out of irresponsibility and disposed of when deemed an inconvenience? Where they are abandoned, neglected, or aborted? Where they can be turned into warriors, trafficked, or used as slaves to turn a profit? Where children are often malnourished, fatherless, ignored, and directionless? In such a world we may never find the moral courage to deal with the issues raised in this chapter. But let's at least acknowledge that a part of our responsibility to the next generation is to leave to them a creation that is well cared for so that it can pour into their lives the kind of blessings we have received.

What about the issue of the humane treatment of animals? I am not making an argument against medical research or eating meat. I am suggesting that in these areas and others we should seek to treat animals as humanely as possible. Animals raised for food should not suffer needlessly in the process.

There are other issues in which Scripture calls for the benevolent and respectful stewardship of creation. The purpose here is not to form a political agenda but to work out in our lives what God asks of us. We do these things not because we worship creation but because we worship the One who created the heavens and the earth.

Making It Real

Years ago, I came across a story by a college professor: "I Worried So Much About World Hunger Today that I Went Home and Ate Five Cookies." Kenneth Lundberg describes the frustration he felt about the littered stretch of grass between his office and the place he parked his car that was always strewn with tennis ball containers, sweat socks, candy bar wrappers, beer bottles, pieces of cellophane wrappers, and other litter. Rather than complaining, he decided to take ownership, making a game of it and picking up ten items each way, taking them to his car or his office and throwing them away. Somewhere along the way someone in maintenance became a "silent co-conspirator," placing large orange barrels at each end of the swath. "Finally, the great day arrived when I looked back on my twenty feet of lawn now perfectly clean."

I've done this for several years now. Has general campus appearance changed? Not much! Have litterers stopped littering? No! Then if nothing has changed, why bother?

Here lies the secret. Something has changed. My twenty-foot swath—and me! That five-minute walk is a high spot of the day. Instead of fussing and stewing and storing up negative thoughts, I begin and end my workday in a positive mood. My perspective is brighter. I can enjoy my immediate surroundings—and myself—as I pass through a very special time and space.

My learning—and the twenty-foot swath—does not stop at the building door. There is an important principle that follows wherever I go. I cannot solve man's inhumanity to man, but I can affirm, with a smile and a word of appreciation, those who feel burdened by the need to work at lowly jobs. I cannot right the imbalances of centuries of discrimination, but I can lift up someone who feels the weight of a poor self-image. I can treat women as equals without solving the problems of sex discrimination. I can seek out the social and economic litter in my own twenty-foot swath without demanding of myself that I clean up the whole world.

I now practice a discipline of leaving each time-space capsule of my life a little better than when I entered it. Each personal contact, each event, each room I enter becomes a small challenge. I want to leave it improved, but more important, I am responsible to myself to be improved; and thereby, maybe, just maybe, my having been there will make life better for someone else.

THE IMPORTANCE OF PURPOSE AND MEANING

The Spirit himself testifies with our spirit that we are God's children. Now if we are children, then we are heirs—heirs of God and co-heirs with Christ, if indeed we share in his sufferings in order that we may also share in his glory.
(ROMANS 8:16–17)

A friend of mine describes life as a poker game in which we only have one chip—we need to be very careful about where we lay it down. Grace produces moments in which we can start all over again, but a lot of life can be wasted on the way to that encounter with God.

The late Gordon W. Allport, professor of psychology at Harvard, suggested a set of criteria descriptive of the mature personality—things like the ability to be somewhat objective about oneself, a well-developed sense of humor, and most important, a unifying philosophy of life. "Maturity requires . . . a clear comprehension of life's purpose in terms of an intelligible theory. Or, in brief, some form of unifying philosophy of life." A sense of life's purpose is also foundational to our sense of well-being. We are meaning-seeking creatures and life becomes arduous, even intolerable when we have nothing to aim at, no goal to pursue. Like playing basketball without a hoop or hockey without a goal, the game quickly becomes meaningless and frustrating. Life without purpose makes no sense to us.

Viktor Frankl, the Austrian neurologist, psychiatrist, and Auschwitz survivor whose story was referred to earlier, developed logotherapy (literally, "word" or "meaning" therapy) out of his experiences in the concentration camp. He realized that prisoners with a reason to live were more likely to survive. He later would ask suicidal patients what kept them from killing themselves, and would help them weave the strands of reasons to live into a cord of meaning able to support life.

We all yearn for answers to the fundamental questions of life. Who am I? Where did I come from? What is the purpose of my life? Is this present life all there is to my existence? Is death the final word?

It's important to be careful and truthful when we try to answer these questions of purpose. To say that we ought to just pick something to shoot at, that to have some goal is better than no goal at all, is a grinding half-truth. All too often great pain and tragedy are the consequence of our failure to gain adequate understanding of our true purpose. For example, a person who succeeds in business at the cost of alienating his children and neglecting his or her spouse, or a leader who succeeds politically and financially at the expense of his or her integrity and credibility, are examples of what might be called successful failures. They have succeeded in what they set out to do, but ultimately failed because of an inadequate grasp of the purpose of the thing.

This was the predicament of the rich fool in Jesus' parable in Luke 12:13–21. Jesus told the story of a man whose farming venture was so successful that he eventually had to tear down his old barns and build bigger ones. He says to himself: "You have plenty of grain laid up for many years. Take life easy; eat, drink and be merry." In the end, we find that though he succeeds in all he sets out to do, he fails at life because he fails to discern life's purpose.

Jesus told this parable because a young man had asked him to intervene on his behalf so that he could receive an inheritance he believed he deserved. Seems harmless enough. But Jesus' response was clear, if not harsh. He told the parable of the rich fool to make the crowd aware of the devastating effects of faulty presuppositions about the meaning and purpose of life. *You want me to settle a family dispute about money, not knowing that I can answer and fulfill the deepest needs you have. Never before have you met someone who can forgive your sins, and overcome the seeming finality of death, and restore you to your relationship with your heavenly Father and Creator. And yet you come asking only for money.*

The man in the parable expresses three common presuppositions. First, *he forgets God*. Like the fool of Psalms 14 and 53, he doesn't care what God thinks. God doesn't matter. Look at the story. He says, "I . . . I . . . my . . . I'll . . . I . . . my . . . I . . . myself . . ." In the parable, Jesus begins his response, "But God said . . ."

Second, *he forgets that life has limits*. When we are young it can seem like we have forever to live. This man is not living in the moment but for the future, for the "many years" yet to come. "But God said to him, 'You fool! This very night your life will be demanded from you.'" Life is a gift we receive a moment at a time. We do not have the last seven days. They are gone forever. Tomorrow is not yet here and we may not see it. We have this moment, today, in which to love God, to love people, and to live for the things that matter.

Third, *he stakes his happiness in materialism*, a philosophy that can never satisfy. But God tells him: "This very night your life will be demanded from you. Then who will get what you have prepared for yourself?" Jesus ends, "This is how it will be with whoever stores up things for themselves but is not rich toward God." Materialism is not congruent with our deepest needs and leads to wasting our lives.

Progress is more than just movement. It is movement in the right direction, the one set for us by God, and our purpose determines our direction. Getting from point A to point B may not be progress at all if we eventually discover that the purpose of life was to get to point C.

These essential questions of life and destiny have had many possible answers offered over the centuries. One measure of the validity of the answers is how they address our deepest needs. Truth is by its nature liberating and life-giving. It provides an accurate map for making choices about how to live. What good are our philosophies if they do not squarely address what's really going on inside of us? One of the most compelling arguments for the truthfulness of Jesus' teaching is the way it corresponds with gritty reality, the way it so perfectly fits like hand in glove with the deepest human need. There is an amazing coherence in his answers to these crucial questions. Because he knows who we are, Jesus consistently leads us to ultimate reality. He shows us how to live in the context of things as they really are.

Who Am I? Where Did I Come From?

Only God can tell us who we are.

David wrote:

> For you created my inmost being;
> you knit me together in my mother's womb.
> I praise you because I am fearfully and wonderfully made;
> your works are wonderful,
> I know that full well.
>
> My frame was not hidden from you
> when I was made in the secret place,
> when I was woven together in the depths of the earth.
>
> Your eyes saw my unformed body;
> all the days ordained for me
> were written in your book
> before one of them came to be.
> (Psalm 139:13–16)

Before you existed as a single cell, God already knew you and loved you, and wrote a multi-volume book about your life. Before you had a physical existence, you had a history with God in the mind of God in which you already mattered to him.

It's easy to think of ourselves as pursuing and finding God. But the truth is he has been in hot pursuit of you your whole life. He has never taken his eye off you, never given up on you. Ultimately he chose you, loved you, and died for you long before you ever gave him a single thought.

When we come to Jesus with our sin and need and invite his grace, we are restored to a relationship with God, a relationship that fits seamlessly with the inward realities that drive us. We belong to him. Our lives will never make much sense until we figure that out.

One of the things that I have done at times over the years is to recite to my children the stories of the days they were born. I describe the events with careful detail, explaining our emotions throughout the day, especially as they were born and we held them for the first time. We may be sitting at home or riding in the car and I will just launch into the story. This is one of my idiosyncrasies of which they seem to have never tired. I love to watch them react as I tell their stories. Especially when they were young, each of them had favorite parts that I must not leave out. Brendan enjoyed the end of his birth story best. As I arrived at that part of the story, he would always get a look of enthusiasm that said, "I love this part." The end of his story goes like this: "It was almost midnight and I was about to leave the hospital and go home. I decided to go to the nursery to see you one more time. When I got there, the nursery was full but you were front and center and the nurse was taking care of you. A number of people were standing there and several commented on how cute you were. As I stood there I felt so much love and joy that I thought my chest was going to explode, and I pointed to you and I said, 'That's my boy. That's my boy.' "

Years ago, in Gordon Dalbey's excellent book *Healing the Masculine Soul,* I read that the thing sons most need to hear from their fathers is not the words "I love you," but the words "You are my son. You belong to me."

A few years ago, I took Brendan with me to visit someone in the hospital. As we walked holding hands, I said to Brendan, "I love you, buddy. You are so precious to me. I am so glad that you are my son." Brendan, who was about six, stopped dead in his tracks, looked up at me and said, "I love it when you say that." Now, I had made several statements and wanted to be clear about what he meant. So I asked, "When I say what?" to which he replied, "When you say what you just said. 'You are my son.' "

"See what great love the Father has lavished on us, that we should be called children of God! And that is what we are!" (1 John 3:1).

What Is the Purpose of Life?

When it comes to meaning and purpose, we live along a continuum. At one end are those who have a distinct sense of purpose. In the middle are those who are frustrated in their pursuit of meaning and purpose but have not yet given up. And toward the other end are those who have resigned themselves to purposelessness and futility.

The Bible describes the purpose of life in several ways.

Generally, the purpose of my life is *to glorify God*. A tree glorifies God by pointing creation to the heavens, by reflecting something of his majesty, by being tree-like (Psalm 19:1). Similarly, as beings created in the image of God, we glorify him by living lives that reflect his image.

Ultimately, our purpose is *to become what he created us to be*, working out the grace within and learning to live out the reality of being a new creation. We are called to be "conformed to the image of his Son" (Romans 8:28–29), to "grow to become in every respect the mature body of him who is the head, that is, Christ" (Ephesians 4:11–16).

Specifically, we are called *to live in the kingdom of God* and to engage in kingdom-building activity. We are to sense what matters to God and what he is doing in the world, and to dig ourselves deeply into those things. We are to do what God wants done and participate in the unfolding of God's plan. On one occasion the disciples were concerned because Jesus had not had anything to eat. They were surprised when he told them that in fact he already had some food. "My food," said Jesus, "is to do the will of him who sent me and to finish his work" (John 4:34).

I have always found real comfort in the way Jesus described his reasons for coming to be with us. Jesus, asking a Samaritan woman for a drink, explained what he called "living water." He said, "Everyone who drinks this water will be thirsty again, but whoever drinks the water I give him will never thirst. Indeed, *the water I give them will become in them a spring of water welling up to eternal life*" (John 4:13–14). Later, John wrote, "On the last and greatest day of the festival, Jesus stood and said in a loud voice, 'Let anyone who is thirsty come to me and drink. *Whoever believes in me, as Scripture has said, streams of living water will flow from within them*'" (John 7:37–38). Again, describing himself as "the good shepherd," he said, "The thief comes only to steal and kill and destroy; *I have come that they may have life, and have it to the full*" (John 10:10). Jesus came to move us from emptiness and futility to fullness, purpose, and joy. And there is no place of greater contentment than the one we find in knowing that we are doing what we were created to do.

Is Death the Final Word on Human Existence?

The problem of death is huge for us as humans. This book has focused on how to live well, but we all know the truth. No matter how well we live, we will still die someday. We are the only creatures on the planet aware of our impending death. The writer of Ecclesiastes says that God has "set eternity in the human heart" (3:11)—that insatiable hunger for something more, that inability to believe this life is all there is.

William James described death as "the worm at the core" of human pretense to happiness. The apostle Paul described death as an enemy, "the last enemy" to be destroyed. The writer of Hebrews describes us as held in slavery by our fear of death (Hebrews 2:9, 14–18). George Wald, the Nobel Prize–winning scientist, talked about our inability to face death. He confessed that at sixty-nine he had never seen a person born and had never seen a person die, wondering how we can hope to live emotionally healthy lives when the kinds of events that are sources of our deepest human emotion have all but been expunged from our experience. Max Lucado speaks of death as a lump under the carpet, the last thing any of us wants to talk about. When was the last time any of us in a casual conversation asked someone how they were feeling about their inevitable death?

Death stares us all in the face. It makes it hard to feel hopeful about the future.

The big question is whether there is any reasonable hope for us in the face of death. The Christian answer is "Yes!" The message is a very simple one and is summarized by Paul in 1 Corinthians 15:1–3:

> Now, brothers and sisters, I want to remind you of the gospel I preached to you, which you received and on which you have taken your stand. . . . For what I received I passed on to you as of first importance: that Christ died for our sins according to the Scriptures, that he was buried, that he was raised on the third day according to the Scriptures.

By "first importance," Paul means this is the most important message we will ever hear. The word *gospel* means "good news" or that this is the best news we will ever hear. And yet the message is so simple:

Jesus died.

He was so completely dead that they buried him.

He rose again on the third day.

God assumes our humanity in the incarnation, lives with us, and dies in our place. In painful, cruel, sin-bearing death, Jesus destroys the power of sin, and in his resurrection he breaks the power of death. Then, in his amazing grace and generosity, he shares that victory with anyone willing to follow him. There is hope for us—the grace of God made available through the death and resurrection of Jesus Christ.

If that is true, then it really is the best and most important news we will ever hear.

As a physician, I have found great joy in delivering babies. At times I have been so overwhelmed with the joy of this miracle that I have cried as I experience the crowning of the head and then a human life passing into my hands as it enters the world. This can be embarrassing—when the mother is not crying, the father is not crying, and the nurse is not crying, but the doctor . . .

I have often thought of how much the way we enter this world mirrors our experience at the end of life. Others have explained it well and I am particularly fond of this description by Philip Yancey:

> Your world (in the womb) is dark, safe, secure. You are bathed in warm liquid, cushioned from shock. You do nothing for yourself; you are fed automatically, and a murmuring heartbeat assures you that someone larger than you fills all your needs. . . . You meet no sharp objects, no pain, no threatening adventures. A fine existence.
>
> One day you feel a tug. The walls begin falling in on you. Those soft cushions are now pulsing and beating against you, crushing you downward. Your body is bent double, your limbs twisted and wrenched. You're falling, upside down. For the first time in your life, you feel pain. . . . There is more pressure, almost too intense to bear. Your head is squeezed flat, and you are pushed harder, harder into a dark tunnel. Oh, the pain. Noise. More pressure.
>
> You hurt all over. You hear a groaning sound and an awful, sudden fear rushes in on you. It is happening—your world is collapsing. You're sure it's the end. You see a piercing, blinding light. Cold, rough hands pull at you. Waaaaahhhhh!
>
> Congratulations, you have just been born.
>
> Death is like that. On this end it seems so fearsome . . . full of pain. But beyond the darkness and pain there's a whole new world outside. . . .

Confusing Religion With Purpose

Gordon W. Allport raises the possibility that for many people religion may not provide purpose or a unifying philosophy of life. He suggests two reasons for this. First, some people may find this unifying philosophy in some standard clarification of values other than religion. Second, Allport reminds us that religious sentiment does not in itself necessarily fulfill the criteria for a mature, integrated personality. I would add to the discussion the possibility that our experience of religion is a far cry from a real relationship with God in which true purpose can be found.

The religious sentiments of many people—perhaps of most people—are decidedly immature. Often they are holdovers from childhood. They are self-centered constructions in which a deity is adopted who favors the immediate interests of the individual, like a Santa Claus or an overindulgent father. Or the sentiment may be of a tribal sort: "My church is better than your church. God prefers my people to your people." In cases of this sort, religion merely serves self-esteem. It is utilitarian and incidental in the life. It is a defense mechanism (often an escape mechanism) and does not embrace and guide the life as a whole. It is an "extrinsic" value in the sense that the person finds it "useful" in serving his immediate ends.

This "use" of faith, "extrinsic" faith, is a reflection of the tendency to make choices on the basis of what we believe will lead to personal satisfaction, choices often made without an adequate reference point. The purpose of such religion is to make us happy. It is not comprehensive or integrative. It serves us as it suits us. In no way does it provide a unifying philosophy of life. It is possible, and perhaps often the case, that very religious people can remain decidedly immature.

On the other hand, Allport suggests that for many, religious sentiment may reflect "a carefully chosen, mature, and productive philosophy of life," providing a solution to life's puzzles. Allport indicates that this kind of faith occurs when the individual surrenders to this purpose rather than "using" it, when religion becomes an "intrinsic" value that is comprehensive, integrative, and motivational. In other words, when you allow your faith to become a deep, influential part of you.

Jonathan Edwards endeavored to describe the nature of true religious experience in *A Treatise Concerning Religious Affections*. Edwards was seeking to understand why many people who appeared deeply affected by spiritual awakening (during the First Great Awakening in the 1730s and 1740s) showed little real change in their lives years later. What he writes sheds helpful light on the movement, to use Allport's terms, from religion as an "extrinsic" value, which is "used," to religion as an "intrinsic" value, which motivates. He uses the term *affections* to mean our "desires" or "internal motivations," the spring of our actions. Edwards wrote, "He who has only doctrinal knowledge and theory, without affection, is never as engaged in the goodness of faith."

True religion must be psychologically true. Though Edwards distinguishes between worldly and religious affections, the affection that drives us toward self-fulfillment and personal satisfaction is of the same type as the affection that is the catalyst of religious commitment. "Religion is practical," according to Edwards. If we are to affirm that God created us with these affections or desires, then according to Edwards, religion must involve things "such as fear, hope, love, hatred, desire, joy, sorrow, gratitude, compassion, and zeal." It must involve our whole being. It must engage us far more deeply than merely on the level of intellect, or as a device for manipulating circumstances for our personal well-being.

In our choice to follow Jesus, to yield ourselves to his ways and his purposes, to live as he lived in all aspects of his life, faith becomes intrinsic rather than extrinsic. It engages us on the level of our affections, and it becomes "true."

Some people see relationship with God as a safety net. We're walking the tightrope of our accomplishments, successes, family, relationships, health, etc. When things fall apart, God is there to catch us. But the truth about life is that God is the tightrope, the net, the whole system, our very reason for being.

What Really Matters?

The continuous commands in Scripture to love God all-consumingly and to love others sacrificially push us headlong into the things that really matter. They constantly remind us that life is not all about us, bringing tremendous purpose to our lives.

Once again, when it comes to the matter of life's purpose, we find growing evidence within a variety of studies suggesting the positive impact of living with purpose on every aspect of health and well-being—it decreases stress, improves immune response, increases rebound capacity after illness, leads to greater satisfaction with life, and provides many other long-term benefits.

Psychologist Erik Erikson describes stages of psychosocial development through which a healthy developing human should pass between infancy and late adulthood. In each stage the person learns, grows, and develops mastery of a new set of challenges. Each stage builds upon the other, and failure to successfully negotiate any stage may result in problems later in life.

- Hope: Trust vs. Mistrust (Infants, 0 to 1 year)

- Will: Autonomy vs. Shame & Doubt (Toddlers, 2 to 3 years)

- Purpose: Initiative vs. Guilt (Preschool, 4 to 6 years)

- Competence: Industry vs. Inferiority (Childhood, 7 to 12 years)

- Fidelity: Identity vs. Role Confusion (Adolescents, 13 to 19 years)

- Love: Intimacy vs. Isolation (Young Adults, 20 to 34 years)

- Care: Generativity vs. Stagnation (Middle Adulthood, 35 to 65 years)

- Wisdom: Integrity vs. Despair (Seniors, 65 years onward)

Middle adulthood involves a choice between generativity and self-absorption or stagnation. In other words, will we invest in the next generation, pouring what is needed into the lives of younger people, or will we live for ourselves, pursuing the things that will make us happy?

In late adulthood we are faced with the possibility of either integrity or despair. In this context, integrity refers to being whole, sound, and complete. It means looking back on our lives with happiness and contentment, feeling fulfilled, with a deep sense that life has meaning and that we've made a contribution. Integrity leads to an acceptance of death, while despair may cause us to fear death and question the value and meaning of our lives. Implicitly, generativity produces hope and integrity while self-absorption leads to despair.

Shaping our lives in the context of our relationship with God gives rise to the strength and perspective needed to deal with the problems and struggles of growing old. As our physical faculties begin to fail, so may our capacity for certain types of pleasure. The difficulties of old age reveal something about our character. Physical decline exposes that which matters most to us. This inability to continue in the pleasures we have pursued may lead to a sense of loss, resulting in bitterness and disappointment if our happiness is rooted primarily in these pleasures. For aging to engage us in a process of maturing and ripening, we must attend to the needs of the whole self and not just our physical appetites and self-fulfillment.

Aging does not need to be a descent into dullness, boredom, and bitterness. It can be an ascent into excellence, wisdom, and joy if we have invested in what really matters. If our primary love is for God, and we have invested in others, in the next generation, in the things that matter to God, then our latter years may be a period of integrity in which we enjoy those whom we have loved and savor thoughtfully the wonder of the gift of life.

Many people prefer the stark honesty of writers like Jean Paul Sartre and Albert Camus, who describe the emptiness and meaninglessness of life without God. For many, this bleak view of life reflects a deeper sense of reality than the hollow ramblings of some religious people who claim to know God but offer only the same old cultural drivel found everywhere else. Ernest Becker, though not a Christian at the time, wrote something that seems to me a prophetic challenge to the church today:

> The great perplexity of our time, the churning of our age, is that the youth have sensed—for better or for worse—a great social-historical truth: that just as there are useless self-sacrifices in unjust wars, so too is there ignoble heroics of whole societies: It can be the viciously destructive heroics of Hitler's Germany, or the plain debasing and silly heroics of the acquisition and display of consumer goods, the piling up of money and privileges that now characterize whole ways of life. . . .
>
> And the crisis of society is, of course, the crisis of organized religion too: Religion is no longer valid as a hero system, and so youth scorn it. If traditional culture is discredited as heroics, then the church that supports that culture automatically discredits itself. If the church, on the other hand, chooses to insist on its own special heroics, it might find that in crucial ways it must work against the culture, recruit youth to be anti-heroes to the ways of life of the society they live in. This is the dilemma of religion in our time.

A church that merely reinforces the values of the culture, that tells people that the goal of life is to be nice, middle-class people and to pile up as much stuff as we can in the process, offers no real hope that life can be purposeful and meaningful. But when the church takes its own message seriously—that God has come to make all things new, forgiving and transforming us through grace, and that he invites us to participate with him in building his kingdom—we find ourselves connecting with people's soulful longings, the hunger that is such a big part of what makes us human.

Conclusion

When I was a freshman in college, I engaged in an arduous struggle between my desire to study medicine and my sense of call to ministry. I came to see that one of the main reasons I had chosen the pursuit of medicine over ministry at that time was my feelings about growing up with little money. We often struggled, and I felt that I wanted and needed to rise above that. That realization led to a more important struggle over the degree to which I trusted God.

That fall I read through the gospel of Matthew and came upon these words from Jesus: "The student is not above the teacher, nor a servant above his master. It is enough for students to be like their teachers, and servants like their masters" (Matthew 10:24–25). I took two pieces of notebook paper, taped them together, and wrote in large letters, "Is it enough?" Is it enough for me to be like Jesus? He said, "Foxes have dens and birds have nests, but the Son of Man has no place to lay his head" (Matthew 8:20). Is that enough for me? Once I was able to answer that question, the other pieces seemed to fall into place.

Unlike the prophets, Jesus rarely called people out. And when he did, he usually confronted people who thought they didn't have problems. A sense of need was his invitation to friendship. Usually he demonstrated great patience. He reasoned with them. He asked hard questions: What is the purpose of life? What really matters ultimately and eternally? He asked them to look at difficult issues and invited them to take a different perspective on things. He challenged them to do things God's way, to become more than they thought they could be by themselves—a woman caught in adultery offered a new start; fishermen who became fishers of men; Zacchaeus, who changed from shrewd to good.

What do we do with the teachings of Jesus that exceed our experience, that appear too costly, that offend our human sensibilities? Søren Kierkegaard wrote this tongue-in-cheek description of our problem:

> The matter is quite simple. The Bible is very easy to understand. But we Christians are a bunch of scheming swindlers. We pretend to be unable to understand it because we know very well that the minute we understand, we are obliged to act accordingly. Take any words in the New Testament and forget everything except pledging yourself to act accordingly. My God, you will say, if I do that my whole life will be ruined. How would I ever get on in the world? Herein lies the real place of Christian scholarship. Christian scholarship is the Church's

prodigious invention to defend itself against the Bible, to ensure that we can continue to be good Christians without the Bible coming too close. Oh, priceless scholarship, what would we do without you? Dreadful it is to fall into the hands of the living God. Yes, it is even dreadful to be alone with the New Testament.

What has been described within these pages is intended in part to help us understand the reasonableness of what Jesus asks of us. In the end he asks for everything, our whole life, all that we are. And it is the most loving thing he can do. Why is this foundational choice to follow so important?

Because it is the only way that leads to life. According to Jesus:

> Whoever wants to be my disciple must deny themselves and take up their cross daily and follow me. For whoever wants to save their life will lose it, but whoever loses their life for me will save it. What good is it for someone to gain the whole world, and yet lose or forfeit their very self? (Luke 9:23–25)

It is a choice that is spiritually necessary. Jesus explained:

> Enter through the narrow gate. For wide is the gate and broad is the road that leads to destruction, and many enter through it. But small is the gate and narrow the road that leads to life, and only a few find it. (Matthew 7:13–14)

Following Jesus is the safest place for the hurting and struggling. Jesus invites us:

> Come to me, all you who are weary and burdened, and I will give you rest. Take my yoke upon you and learn from me, for I am gentle and humble in heart, and you will find rest for your souls. For my yoke is easy and my burden is light. (Matthew 11:28–30)

And following Jesus puts us on the path to life. He said:

The thief comes only to steal and kill and destroy; I have come that they may have life, and have it to the full. (John 10:10)

In the end many will be tempted to say, *This is not the life I want.* After all, the life to which Jesus calls us is not an easy life. But it is both now and eternally the best possible life.

appendix A

DIFFICULT TEXTS REGARDING
THE LAW IN SCRIPTURE

Some of the most compelling arguments in the recent wave of anti-God literature have to do with some assertions in the Law, texts that by themselves seem to support the institution of slavery (Leviticus 25:44–46; Exodus 21:7–11, 20–21, 26–27. See also Ephesians 6:5 and 1 Timothy 6:1–2) and others that encourage the penalty of death for children who are rebellious (Exodus 21:15; Leviticus 20:9; Deuteronomy 21:18–21; Mark 7:9–13; and Matthew 15:4–7). These texts are important in a discussion of the goodness of God's law and cannot be ignored. The needed discussion of these important issues and their impact on questions of the existence of God, the character of God, and the truth of the Bible are worthy of thorough and lengthy consideration, but that discussion is beyond the scope of this book. The most we can do here is to acknowledge the problem these texts present for many people and point them in a direction that would provide a framework for possible answers.

Many have reasoned that these statements about slavery merely served to bring a small measure of civility to an institution that already existed as a matter of fact. This idea is evidenced in a number of ways. The penalty in the Mosaic Law for kidnapping and enslaving someone was death (Exodus 21:16). Runaway slaves were to go free and were to be allowed to live anywhere they wanted (Deuteronomy 23:15–16).

This argument makes some sense until one asks why a book revealing the character of God could not simply acknowledge slavery as evil and make it clear that it had no place among his people. Part of the answer to this may lie in realizing that the Bible is a record of the process God is engaged in to restore the whole of creation. That salvation history involves a progressive redemption, a process unfolding incrementally, is reflected in Paul's statement that in Christ "there is neither Jew nor Gentile, neither slave nor free, nor is there male and female, for you are all one in Christ Jesus" (Galatians 3:28). Paul describes an agenda that includes the eradication of sexism and slavery through the renewing influence of the gospel in human lives. It appears that he saw himself as having no choice but to focus on the Jew-Gentile problem facing the primitive church, but one senses that given time he would have taken on these other problems as well. Paul's opposition to slavery is further evidenced in this description of the role of the law and the impact of the gospel.

> We know that the law is good if one uses it properly. We also know that the law is made not for the righteous but for lawbreakers and rebels, the ungodly and sinful, the unholy and irreligious, for those who kill their fathers or mothers, for murderers, for the sexually immoral, for those practicing homosexuality, for slave traders and liars and perjurers—and for whatever else is contrary to the sound doctrine that conforms to the gospel concerning the glory of the blessed God, which he entrusted to me. (1 Timothy 1:8–11)

Thankfully, most people responding to the Bible as a whole have energetically engaged in opposing all such practices. Evangelical Christians in England and the United States were at the leading edge of the abolitionist movement. The change of heart and mind in John Newton over many years, and the passion and sacrifice of people like William

Wilberforce grew out of a relationship with God by which they understood the dignity and value of every person. It is estimated that there are over 20 million people in the world today who are living as slaves due to human trafficking in the sex industry, including children, forced laborers known as "bonded laborers," people considered inheritable property, etc. The redemption to which the Bible points has not yet been realized, and the wretched condition of the human soul remains the source of most human suffering.

The question regarding the treatment of children is a far more difficult one. As the verses describe the circumstances in which the penalty was to be applied it is clear that the texts refer to adult children who intentionally harm their parents. Jesus' reference to these laws is intended as a contrast to the glibness with which the Pharisees and teachers of the Law treated the Law of Moses. His answer is not to encourage enforcement of the particular law but to help them understand what their attitude toward the law reveals about the real condition of their hearts.

appendix B

SCRIPTURES REGARDING JOY

The Bible is persistent in its emphasis on God's passionate commitment to our well-being—a well-being usually expressed as joy. Joy is sometimes found in the places we least expect it. This list should help you identify and explore some of those places.

1. Joy Commanded

- Shout for joy to God, all the earth! Sing the glory of his name; make his praise glorious. (Psalm 66:1–2)

- Not only so, but we also glory in our sufferings, because we know that suffering produces perseverance. (Romans 5:3)

- Rejoice with those who rejoice; mourn with those who mourn. (Romans 12:15)

- Rejoice in the Lord always. I will say it again: Rejoice! (Philippians 4:4)

- However, do not rejoice that the spirits submit to you, but rejoice that your names are written in heaven. (Luke 10:20)

2. Joy and God's Presence

- Splendor and majesty are before him; strength and joy are in his dwelling place. (1 Chronicles 16:27)

- You make known to me the path of life; you will fill me with joy in your presence, with eternal pleasures at your right hand. (Psalm 16:11)

- Surely you have granted him unending blessings and made him glad with the joy of your presence. (Psalm 21:6)

- The LORD is my strength and my shield; my heart trusts in him, and he helps me. My heart leaps for joy, and with my song I praise him. (Psalm 28:7)

- Then I will go to the altar of God, to God, my joy and my delight. I will praise you with the lyre, O God, my God. (Psalm 43:4)

- Those the LORD has rescued will return. They will enter Zion with singing; everlasting joy will crown their heads. Gladness and joy will overtake them, and sorrow and sighing will flee away. (Isaiah 35:10)

- Very truly I tell you, you will weep and mourn while the world rejoices. You will grieve, but your grief will turn to joy. (John 16:20)

- Though you have not seen him, you love him; and even though you do not see him now, you believe in him and are filled with an inexpressible and glorious joy. (1 Peter 1:8)

3. Joy and Becoming

- And we know that in all things God works for the good of those who love him, who have been called according to his purpose. For those God foreknew he also predestined to be conformed to the image of his Son, that he might be the firstborn among many brothers and sisters. And those he predestined, he also called; those he called, he also justified; those he justified, he also glorified. (Romans 8:28–30)

- Consider it pure joy, my brothers and sisters, whenever you face trials of many kinds, because you know that the testing of your faith produces perseverance. Let perseverance finish its work so that you may be mature and complete, not lacking anything. (James 1:2–4)

- Then your barns will be filled to overflowing, and your vats will brim over with new wine. My son, do not despise the LORD's discipline, and do not resent his rebuke, because the LORD disciplines those he loves, as a father the son he delights in. Blessed are those who find wisdom, those who gain understanding, for she is more profitable than silver and yields better returns than gold. (Proverbs 3:10–14)

4. Joy and Obedience

- The prospect of the righteous is joy, but the hopes of the wicked come to nothing. (Proverbs 10:28)

- Deceit is in the hearts of those who plot evil, but those who promote peace have joy. (Proverbs 12:20)

- But may the righteous be glad and rejoice before God; may they be happy and joyful. (Psalm 68:3)

5. Joy of Salvation

- Though you have not seen him, you love him; and even though you do not see him now, you believe in him and are filled with an inexpressible and glorious joy, for you are receiving the end result of your faith, the salvation of your souls. (1 Peter 1:8–9)

- Then he calls his friends and neighbors together and says, "Rejoice with me; I have found my lost sheep." I tell you that in the same way there will be more rejoicing in heaven over one sinner who repents than over ninety-nine righteous persons who do not need to repent. . . . In the same way, I tell you, there is rejoicing in the presence of the angels of God over one sinner who repents. . . . "But we had to celebrate and be glad, because this brother of yours was dead and is alive again; he was lost and is found" (Luke 15:6–7, 10, 32).

6. Joy of Creation

- Let the fields be jubilant, and everything in them; let all the trees of the forest sing for joy. (Psalm 96:12)

- Shout for joy to God, all the earth! Sing the glory of his name; make his praise glorious. (Psalm 66:1–2)

- You will go out in joy and be led forth in peace; the mountains and hills will burst into song before you, and all the trees of the field will clap their hands. (Isaiah 55:12)

7. Joy From God

- For seven days celebrate the festival to the LORD your God at the place the LORD will choose. For the LORD your God will bless you in all your harvest and in all the work of your hands, and your joy will be complete. (Deuteronomy 16:15)

- Celebrate annually . . . as the time when the Jews got relief from their enemies, and as the month when their sorrow was turned into joy and their mourning into a day of celebration. [Mordecai] wrote them to observe the days as days of feasting and joy and giving presents of food to one another and gifts to the poor. (Esther 9:21–22)

- Fill my heart with joy when their grain and new wine abound. (Psalm 4:7)

- You turned my wailing into dancing; you removed my sackcloth and clothed me with joy. (Psalm 30:11)

- Restore to me the joy of your salvation and grant me a willing spirit, to sustain me. (Psalm 51:12)

- Satisfy us in the morning with your unfailing love, that we may sing for joy and be glad all our days. (Psalm 90:14)

- The LORD has done it this very day; let us rejoice today and be glad. (Psalm 118:24)

- Let them sacrifice thank offerings and tell of his works with songs of joy. (Psalm 107:22)

- Nehemiah said, "Go and enjoy choice food and sweet drinks, and send some to those who have nothing prepared. This day is holy to our Lord. Do not grieve, for the joy of the LORD is your strength." (Nehemiah 8:10)

- In the midst of a very severe trial, their overflowing joy and their extreme poverty welled up in rich generosity. (2 Corinthians 8:2)

8. Joy and Suffering

- The apostles left the Sanhedrin, rejoicing because they had been counted worthy of suffering disgrace for the Name. (Acts 5:41)

- Not only so, but we also glory in our sufferings, because we know that suffering produces perseverance; perseverance, character; and character, hope. And hope does not put us to shame, because God's love has been poured out into our hearts through the Holy Spirit, who has been given to us. (Romans 5:3–5)

- For the joy set before him he endured the cross. (Hebrews 12:2)

9. Joy in Knowing

- Your statutes are my heritage forever; they are the joy of my heart. (Psalm 119:111)

- But the angel said to them, "Do not be afraid. I bring you good news that will cause great joy for all the people" (Luke 2:10).

- I have told you this so that my joy may be in you and that your joy may be complete. (John 15:11)

- However, do not rejoice that the spirits submit to you, but rejoice that your names are written in heaven. (Luke 10:20)

10. Joy in Others

- Then make my joy complete by being like-minded, having the same love, being one in spirit and of one mind. (Philippians 2:2)

- Therefore, my brothers and sisters, you whom I love and long for, my joy and crown, stand firm in the Lord in this way, dear friends! (Philippians 4:1)

- For what is our hope, our joy, or the crown in which we will glory in the presence of our Lord Jesus when he comes? Is it not you? (1 Thessalonians 2:19)

- Fixing our eyes on Jesus, the pioneer and perfecter of faith. For the joy set before him he endured the cross, scorning its shame, and sat down at the right hand of the throne of God. (Hebrews 12:2)

- Your love has given me great joy and encouragement, because you, brother, have refreshed the hearts of the Lord's people. (Philemon 7)

- It has given me great joy to find some of your children walking in the truth, just as the Father commanded us. (2 John 4)

- I have no greater joy than to hear that my children are walking in the truth. (3 John 4)

- May your fountain be blessed, and may you rejoice in the wife of your youth. (Proverbs 5:18)

- Rejoice with those who rejoice; mourn with those who mourn. (Romans 12:15)

11. Joy as an Inward Reality

- A happy heart makes the face cheerful, but heartache crushes the spirit. (Proverbs 15:13)

- Is anyone among you in trouble? Let them pray. Is anyone happy? Let them sing songs of praise. (James 5:13)

ACKNOWLEDGMENTS

In following you, Jesus, my life has been salvaged and is being renovated at every level. You are the fairest, the kindest, and the best. How can I possibly thank you?

Thank you, Carole, for your love and joy that makes our life together as a family truly wonderful. My sense of awe and respect continue to grow. And thank you, Jonathan, Caitlin, Brendan, and Ciara for your love and support and for so generously sharing yourselves with me and allowing me to tell your stories as well. The privilege of being your father still takes my breath away. I love each of you.

My gratitude to Andy McGuire, who is more than an outstanding editor. You have also been an encourager, cheerleader, and friend. You made this project a lot more fun than it should have been by your joy and warm spirit. I am deeply grateful.

Thanks to the Bethany Church family for your love and support, for your openness to God's work in our lives and for the joy of serving Jesus together in a way that is making a difference in people's lives. I love you all. It is a privilege to be a part of such a community.

Thanks to my patients who teach me new things every day about what it is to be truly human by demonstrating trust and openness. What a precious gift.

Thanks to many who have lived and taught so well—Colin and

Olive Brown, Jim Bradley, Robert Meye, Richard Mouwe, Bob Schaper, Lane Scott, John Hartley, Marianne Campbell, Gladys Jahr, and many others who helped write this book by your investment in me in helping shape my heart and mind.

And I'm grateful for friends like Scott Munroe, Blake Firstman, Anita Lewis, Preedar Oreggio (fellow physician and partner extraordinaire), Frank Schifani, Joe Battaglia, Rush Williams, JoAnne Shepard, and others who have poured their love, support, and prayers into this project. Thanks for caring.

And special thanks to Roger Renner and Jack Carter for generously sharing this amazing chapter in your journey with me. Your faith and courage challenge me and lift my spirits every day. I love you both.

I am genuinely humbled to be part of such an incredible team.

NOTES

Introduction

p. 13   "These directions for living reveal his grace . . ." See Appendix A.

p. 14   "Scripture contains the perfect rule . . ." John Calvin, *The Epistles of Paul to Timothy and Titus* (Edinburgh: Oliver and Boyd, 1964), 330.

Chapter 1: Diagnosing the Problem

p. 23   "Why do we do what we do?" Ernest Becker, *The Denial of Death* (New York: Free Press, 1973), 5–8. Becker, too, raises the issue of the importance of grasping the fundamental nature of the human dilemma. "For twenty-five hundred years we have hoped and believed that if mankind could reveal itself to itself, could widely come to know its own cherished motives, then somehow it would tilt the balance in its own favor."

p. 25   "I was under no compulsion of need . . ." Augustine, *The Confessions* (Hyde Park: New City Press, 1997), 37.

p. 26   "There is something within each person . . ." Solomon Schimmel, in his excellent book *The Seven Deadly Sins: Jewish, Christian, and Classical Reflections on Human Psychology* (New York: Oxford University Press, 1997), 226, explains that "the scientific advances of the twentieth century, based on determinism as a working model of human nature, have vastly increased our ability to predict individual and group behavior. So it is reasonable, psychologists say, to assume that the determinist model is more accurate than the free-will one. The adoption of a determinist model has profound implications for our notions of sin, vice, crime, responsibility, guilt, blame, and punishment."

p. 26   "It was granted to me to carry away . . . " Alexander I. Solzhenitsyn, *The Gulag Archipelago* (New York: Harper & Row, 1975), 615–616.

p. 27   "What else does this craving . . . " Blaise Pascal, *Pensees* (New York: Penguin Books, 1966), 75.

p. 28   "The root of our problem . . . " Paul Achtemeier, *Romans: Interpretation, A Bible Commentary for Teaching and Preaching* (Louisville: John Knox Press, 1985), 66.

p. 28   "A car is made to run on gasoline . . . " C. S. Lewis, *Mere Christianity* (New York: Macmillan, 1952), 54.

p. 29   "I am not being flippant when I say that all of us suffer . . . " Gerald G. May, MD, *Addiction and Grace: Love and Spirituality in the Healing of Addictions* (San Francisco: Harper, 1988), 3–4.

p. 32   "What will come of what I do . . . " Leo Tolstoy, *Confession*, trans. David Patterson (New York: W. W. Norton, 1983), 34–35.

p. 33   ". . . to the biblical description of the fall." See John Stott's discussion of the historicity of Adam and Eve. He writes, "Scripture clearly intends us to accept their historicity as the original human pair." He proceeds to summarize the biblical evidence for this view. John Stott, *Romans: Good News for the World* (Downers Grove, IL: InterVarsity Press, 1994), 162–166.

p. 34   "So much of life's suffering could be eliminated . . . " The whole question of reliability or validity is one that will cause no end of debate and consternation. At the heart of this discussion is the validation of many aspects of biblical morality by the sciences.

p. 34   "The old Chinese were right . . . " This story is related by Jacques Ellul in *Reason for Being: A Meditation on Ecclesiastes*, trans. Joyce Main Hanks (Grand Rapids: Eerdmans, 1990), 128.

p. 35   "The principal point . . . of the law . . . " Martin Luther, *A Commentary on St. Paul's Epistle to the Galatians* (1531; James Clarke, 1953), 316.

p. 35   "Nothing can be more cruel . . . " Dietrich Bonhoeffer, *Life Together*, trans. John W. Doberstein (New York: Harper & Row, 1954), 107.

p. 35   "Perhaps the main task of the minister . . . " Henri J. M. Nouwen, *The Wounded Healer* (Garden City, New York: Image Books, 1979), 93.

p. 36   "For several decades we psychologists . . . " O. Hobart Mowrer, "Sin, the Lesser of Two Evils," *American Psychologist*, XV (1960): 303.

p. 36   "Healthy-mindedness is inadequate as a philosophical doctrine . . ." William James, *The Varieties of Religious Experience* (New York: Penguin Books, 1982), 163.

p. 37   "Recovery (constructive change, redemption) . . . " Mowrer, 304.

pp. 37–38   "Present-day psychology and psychiatry . . . " Donald Campbell, "On the Conflicts Between Biological and Social Evolution and Between Psychology and Moral Tradition," *American Psychologist* (1975): 1103–1104.

p. 38   "on purely scientific grounds, these recipes for living . . ." Campbell, 1103.

p. 38   "since this matter of man's total adjustment . . . " Mowrer, 303.

Chapter 2: Why Forgive?

p. 43   "If God and Israel are husband and wife . . . " Moshe Halbertal and Avishai Margalit, *Idolatry* (Cambridge, MA: Harvard University Press, 1992), 18–19.

p. 43   "possibly the most important single paragraph . . . " Leon Morris, *The Epistle to the Romans* (Grand Rapids: Eerdmans, 1988), 173.

p. 44   "a righteous God righteously 'righteouses' . . . " John Stott, *Romans*, 115. See also Charles E. B. Cranfield, *A Critical and Exegetical Commentary on the Epistle to the Romans* (Edinburgh: T. & T. Clark Publishers, 1975), 217.

p. 45   "The promise of glory is the promise . . . " C. S. Lewis, *The Weight of Glory* (HarperSanFrancisco, 1976), 38–39.

p. 47   "To give up one's pretentions . . . " William James, *Principles of Psychology*, Vol. 1 (Cambridge: Oxford University Press, 1981), 296–297.

p. 48   ". . . shaped by what happens from this moment . . ." See T. W. Manson, *The Sayings of Jesus* (London: SCM Press Ltd., 1949), 312.

p. 49   "Religion operates on the principle . . ." Timothy Keller, *The Reason for God* (New York: Penguin Group, 2008), 186.

p. 50   "Everyone says forgiveness is a lovely idea . . . " C. S. Lewis, *Mere Christianity* (New York: Macmillan, 1952), 104.

p. 50   "I will take the loss . . . " G. B. Caird, *Principalities and Powers: A Study in Pauline Theology* (London: Oxford University Press, 1956), 98.

p. 50   ". . . letting go of our hurt, anger, and desire for revenge." This definition of forgiveness is consistent with many researchers on the subject of forgiveness. Loren L. Toussaint, David R. Williams, Mark A. Musick, Susan A. Everson, "Forgiveness and Health: Age Differences in a U.S. Probability Sample," *Journal of Adult Development* 8 (2001): 250.

pp. 52–53   "Four years later, word reached me that my mother's attacker had been prematurely released . . . " Used with permission from Life Water International and Deleo Moses Ocen.

p. 53   "By refusing and clinging to our unforgiveness . . . " See similar discussion in Philip Carlson, *You Were Made for Love: Embracing the Life You Were Meant to Live* (Colorado Springs: David C. Cook, 2006), 211–213.

p. 53   "The only way to heal the pain . . . " Lewis B. Smedes, *Forgive and Forget: Healing the Hurts We Don't Deserve* (New York: Pocket Books, 1984), 170.

p. 54   "There are a number of dimensions of forgiveness . . . " Toussaint et al., "Forgiveness and Health," 250.

p. 54   "giving up one's right to retribution . . . " Toussaint et al., "Forgiveness and Health," 250.

p. 54   "a conscious, willful and moral act . . . " Cydney J. Van Dyke and Maurice J. Elias, "How Forgiveness, Purpose and Religiosity Are Related to Mental Health and Well-Being of Youth: A review of the literature," *Mental Health, Religion and Culture* 10 (2007): 397.

p. 54   "though forgiveness has been explored by psychologists . . . " Thomas W. Baskin and Robert D. Enright, "Intervention Studies on Forgiveness: A Meta-Analysis," *Journal of Counseling and Development* 82 (2004): 79–90.

p. 54   "Forgiveness leads to decreased depression . . . " Toussaint et al., "Forgiveness and Health," 252–253.

p. 54   "Also, those who are engaged in learning how to forgive . . . " Everett L. Worthington and Michael Scherer, "Forgiveness Is an Emotion-Focused Coping Strategy that Can Reduce Health Risks and Promote Health Resilience: Theory, Review and Hypothesis," *Psychology and Health* 19 (2004): 388–389. J. Pingleton, "The Role and Function of Forgiveness in the Psychotherapeutic Process," *Journal of Psychology and Theology* 17 (1989): 27–35.

Summarized in Toussaint et al., "Forgiveness and Health," 250. Everett L. Worthington Jr., Charlotte van Oyen Witvliet, Pietro Pietrini, Andrea J. Miller, "Forgiveness, Health and Well-Being: A Review of Evidence for Emotional Versus Decisional Forgiveness, Dispositional Forgiveness and Reduced Unforgiveness," *Journal of Behavioral Medicine* 30 (2007): 299. Michael McCullough, "The Power of Forgiveness," *Men's Health* 23 (2008): 42.

p. 55   "forgiveness is associated with social competence . . . " Van Dyke and Elias, "How Forgiveness, Purpose and Religiosity Are Related to Mental Health," 402.

p. 55   "Forgiveness decreases levels of depression . . . " Van Dyke and Elias, "How Forgiveness, Purpose and Religiosity Are Related to Mental Health," 400–403. Also see the excellent review of previous studies by Thomas W. Baskin and Robert D. Enright, "Intervention Studies on Forgiveness: A Meta-Analysis," 79–90.

p. 55   "Undergraduates who had difficulty letting go of anger . . . " See summary of the literature in Van Dyke and Elias, "How Forgiveness, Purpose and Religiosity Are Related to Mental Health," 395–415.

p. 55   "If this stage is not resolved successfully . . . " Neal Krause and Christopher G. Ellison, "Forgiveness by God, Forgiveness of Others, and Psychological Well-Being in Late Life," *Journal for the Scientific Study of Religion* 42 (2003): 79.

p. 55   "One of the key developmental tasks in the life-review process . . . " Robert N. Butler and Myrna I. Lewis, *Aging and Mental Health* (St. Louis: C. V. Mosby, 1982), 326.

p. 56   "Also, older people who forgive . . . " Krause and Ellison, "Forgiveness," 85–86. Consistent with the study by Toussaint et al. (2001), forgiveness of others seems to have a stronger relationship with psychological health than forgiveness by God.

p. 56   ". . . forgiveness protects people from heart disease . . . " B. Kaplan, "Social Health and the Forgiving Heart: The Type B Story," *Journal of Behavioral Medicine* 15 (1992): 3–14. Summarized in Toussaint et al., "Forgiveness and Health," 250.

p. 56   ". . . lowers blood pressure and heart rate." K. Lawler, J. Younger, R. Piferi, E. Billington, R. Jobe, K. Edmondson, W. Jones, "A Change of Heart: Cardiovascular Correlates of Forgiveness in Response to Interpersonal Conflict," *Journal of Behavioral Medicine* 26 (2003): 383.

p. 56   ". . . there was a significant increase in blood flow . . . " Martina A. Waltman, Douglas R. Russell, Catherine T. Coyle, Robert D.

Enright, Anthony C. Holter, and Christopher M. Swoboda, "The Effects of a Forgiveness Intervention on Patients with Coronary Artery Disease," *Psychology and Health* 24 (2009): 11–27.

p. 56   ". . . role in recovery from cancer . . . " J. Pingleton, "The Role and Function of Forgiveness in the Psychotherapeutic Process," *Journal of Psychology and Theology* 17 (1989): 27–35. Summarized in Toussaint et al., "Forgiveness and Health," 250.

p. 56   ". . . decrease in somatic pain." Everett L. Worthington Jr., Charlotte Van Oyen Witvliet, Pietro Pietrini, Andrea J. Miller, "Forgiveness, Health and Well-Being: A Review of Evidence for Emotional Versus Decisional Forgiveness, Dispositional Forgiveness, and Reduced Unforgiveness," *Journal of Behavioral Medicine* 30 (2007): 299. Michael McCullough, "The Power of Forgiveness," *Men's Health* 23 (2008): 42.

p. 56   ". . . clear correlation between forgiveness and five measures of health . . ." K. Lawler, J. Younger, R. Piferi, R. Jobe, K. Edmondson, W. Jones, "The Unique Effects of Forgiveness on Health," *Journal of Behavioral Medicine* 28 (2005): 157–167.

p. 56   "It can cause the kinds of hormonal patterns . . . " Everett L. Worthington, and Michael Scherer, "Forgiveness Is an Emotion-Focused Coping Strategy that Can Reduce Health Risks and Promote Health Resilience: Theory, Review and Hypothesis," *Psychology and Health* 19 (2004): 388–389.

Chapter 3: Gratitude and Happiness

p. 59   ". . . happiness as a 'moral obligation.' " Dennis Prager, *Happiness Is a Serious Problem: A Human Nature Repair Manual* (New York: Regan Books, 1998), 3–4.

p. 59   "Happy people bless others . . . " On the other hand, a recent edition of *Psychology Today* focused on the idea that there are aspects of depression that are actually contagious, passed on through social interaction in families and close relationships. See Michael Yapko, "Secondhand Blues," *Psychology Today* 42 (2009): 87–93.

p. 60   "Melancholy should be an innocent interlude . . . " G. K. Chesterton, *Orthodoxy* (New York: Image Books, 1959), 159.

p. 60   "All men seek happiness . . . " Blaise Pascal, *Pensees*, trans. A .J. Krailsheimer (New York: Penguin Books), 74.

p. 60   "If we were to ask the question . . . " William James, *The Varieties of Religious Experience,* 78.

p. 64   "So I decided to look at the situation . . . " Anwar Sadat, *Anwar el-Sadat: In Search of Identity* (New York: Harper Colophon Books, 1977), 303–304.

p. 64   " . . . Scripture connects these relationships with happiness." See Appendix B, Scriptures Regarding Joy.

p. 66   "Happiness is also related to our capacity . . ." A. H. Maslow, *Motivation and Personality* (New York: Harper, 1954).

p. 69   ". . . grateful people . . . have a greater sense of well-being." Joan Borysenko, "Practicing Gratitude," *Prevention* 56 (2004): 93–95. Loren Toussaint and Philip Friedman, "Forgiveness, Gratitude, and Well-Being: The Mediating Roles of Affect and Beliefs," *Journal of Happiness Studies* 10 (2009): 635–654. Robert A. Emmons and Michael E. McCullough, "Counting Blessings Versus Burdens: An Experimental Investigation of Gratitude and Subjective Well-Being in Daily Life," *Journal of Personality and Social Psychology* 84 (2003): 377–389.

p. 69   "Grateful people are happier people." Robert Emmons, PhD, *Thanks! How Practicing Gratitude Can Make You Happier* (New York: Houghton Mifflin, 2008).

p. 69   "People who feel a sense of connection with other people . . . " Neal Krause and Christopher G. Ellison, "Social Environment of the Church and Feelings of Gratitude Toward God," *Psychology of Religion and Spirituality* 1 (2009): 191.

p. 69   "Spiritually or religiously inclined people . . . " Robert A. Emmons and Teresa T. Kneezel, "Giving Thanks: Spiritual and Religious Correlates of Gratitude," *Journal of Psychology and Christianity* 24 (2005):140–148.

p. 69   ". . . that we can make people healthier . . . " R. Veenhoven, "Healthy Happiness: Effects of Happiness on Physical Health and the Consequences for Preventative Healthcare," *Journal of Happiness Studies* 9 (2008): 449–469.

pp. 69–70 "I have lived by a feeding tube . . . " Used with permission from Dr. Robert Meye.

Chapter 4: Sex

p. 76   "Sex was made for marriage . . . " The goal here is not to provide a biblical exploration of marriage and its importance. This has been done well elsewhere. See for example, *The Mystery of Marriage* by Mike Mason (Portland, OR: Multnomah Press, 1985).

p. 80   "And as he heals, we discover love . . . " Remember, Jesus lived a life of joy and wholeness as a single person.

p. 80   "With all the intentional efforts to avoid judgmental language . . . " For example, see Alison Hipwell, Kate Keenan, Rolf Loeber, and Deena Battista, "Early Predictors of Sexually Intimate Behaviors in an Urban Sample of Young Girls," *Developmental Psychology* 46 (2010): 366–378; and Samuel Onasanya, Iwokwagh Nicholas, and Esther Onasanya, "Influence of the Internet on the Sexual Health of University Undergraduates in Makurdi, Nigeria," *The Nigerian Journal of Guidance and Counseling* 13 (2008): 41–53.

p. 80   "Living together before marriage . . . " Anita Jose, Daniel O'Leary, and Anne Moyer, "Does Premarital Cohabitation Predict Subsequent Marital Stability and Quality? A Meta-Analysis," *Journal of Marriage and Family* 72 (2010): 105–116.

p. 81   "And cohabitating couples had a five times greater . . . " Jeannine Lee, "Cohabitation and Relationship Success" (2008). *www .fisherdivorcerecovery.com/Articles/cohab-full.shtml* provides a good review of some of the relevant research. Even those studies indicating decreased negative effects if the cohabitation occurs during engagement suggest that commitment is crucial to a healthful context for sex. See Galena H. Kline, Scott M. Stanley, Howard J. Markman, P. Antonio Olmos-Gallo, Michelle St. Peters, Sarah W. Whitton, and Lydia Prado, "Timing Is Everything: Pre-Engagement Cohabitation and Increased Risk for Poor Marital Outcomes," *Journal of Family Psychology* 18 (2004): 311–318. Also, Galena Rhoades, Scott M. Stanley, and Howard J. Markman, "The Pre-Engagement Cohabitation Effect: A Replication and Extension of Previous Findings," *Journal of Family Psychology* 23 (2009): 107–111.

p. 81   "Risky behaviors are increasingly understood . . . " See the summary of D. Hallfors, "Teen Sex and Drug-Use Raises Depression Risk Rather Than the Reverse," in *American Journal of Preventive Medicine* 29 (2005) by Jennifer Warner and Michael W. Smith, MD, in WebMD, "Depression Often Follows Risky Teen Behavior" (2005). Also see Karen S. Peterson, "Study Links Depression, Suicide Rates to Teen Sex," *www.usatoday.com/news/health/2003–06–03-teen -usat_x.htm*.

Chapter 5: Love, Commitment, and Family
p. 86   "The portrayal of God as a father who waits . . . " See Helmut Thielicke, *The Waiting Father*, trans. John W. Doberstein (New York: Harper & Row, 1957), 17–29, for an outstanding exposition of this parable and theme.

p. 89   "Psychology has become a religion . . . " Paul C. Vitz, *Psychology As Religion: The Cult of Self-Worship* (Grand Rapids: Eerdmans, 1977), 9–10.

p. 89   "For selfists there seem to be no acceptable duties . . . " Vitz, *Psychology As Religion*, 38.

pp. 89–90   "In your love you see only . . . " Dietrich Bonhoeffer, *Letters and Papers From Prison*, ed. Eberhard Bethge (New York: Macmillan, 1972), 43 (emphasis added).

p. 90   "Love is what you've been through . . . " Quoted by James Thurber, *Life* magazine, March 14, 1960.

p. 92   "Divorce is also associated with a decrease in healthy behaviors . . . " "Marriage and Men's Health," *Harvard Men's Health Watch* (2010) 14: 1–3. Also see Viola Polomeno, "Marriage, Parenthood, and Divorce: Understanding the Past as We Move into the Future," *International Journal of Childbirth Education* (2007) 22: 13–19. In this article, she summarizes conclusions from K. Briggs, W. Denton, S. Johnson, J. Landau, J. Morris, D. Schnarch, and J. Serovich, *Relationships, Health and Marriage: Final Report of the Task Force for Marriage and Family Therapy* (Alexandria, VA: American Association for Marriage and Family Therapy, 2005); R. Erber and M. Wang Erber, *Intimate Relationships: Issues, Theories and Research* (Boston: Allyn and Bacon, 2001); J. K. Kiecolt-Glaser and T. L. Newton, "Marriage and Health: His and Hers," *Psychological Bulletin* (2001) 127: 472–503; S. S. Larson, D. B. Larson, and J. P. Swyers, "Does Divorce Take a Clinical Toll? A research review of potential physical and emotional health risks for adults and children," *Marriage and Family: A Christian Journal* (1999) 2: 105–121.

p. 93   "They are more prone to earlier sexual activity . . . " See Polomeno, "Marriage, Parenthood, and Divorce," 15. Also, P. R. Amato, B. Keith, "Parental Divorce and the Well-Being of Children: A Meta-Analysis," *Psychological Bulletin* (1991) 1110: 26–46; J. S. Wallerstein, "The Long-Term Effects of Divorce on Children: A Review," *Journal of the American Academy of Child and Adolescent Psychiatry* (1991) 30: 349–350; Sharlene A. Wolchick et al., "Six-Year Follow-Up Study of Preventative Interventions for Children of Divorce," *JAMA* (2002) 288: 1874–1881.

p. 93   "Many of these effects may be best explained . . . " Karen DeBord, "Focus on Kids: The Effects of Divorce on Children," published by North Carolina Cooperative Extension Service.

p. 93   "But when divorce happy talk minimizes . . . " Elizabeth Marquardt, *Between Two Worlds: The Inner Lives of Children of Divorce* (New

York: Crown, 2005), 171, as quoted in book review by Gordon E. Finley, "The Myth of the Good Divorce," *PsycCRITIQUES* (2006): 51.

p. 94   "It treats life after divorce as a fun adventure . . . " Discussion of Marquardt's work found in book review by Gordon E. Finley, "The Myth of the Good Divorce" *PsycCRITIQUES* (2006): 51. For other retrospective studies on related topics drawing similar conclusions to Marquardt, see Sanford Braver and William Fabricius at Arizona State University, as summarized in Fabricius (2003); Lisa Laumann-Billings and Robert Emery (2000) at the University of Virginia; and Gordon Finley and Seth Schwartz at Florida International University (Finley & Schwartz, 2006; Schwartz & Finley, 2005).

p. 94   "When the children's relationships with their fathers deteriorated . . . " Constance R. Ahrons, "Family Ties After Divorce: Long-Term Implications for Children," *Family Process* (2006) 46: 53–65.

p. 94   "This loss of well-being . . . " William V. Fabricius and Linda J. Luecken, "Post-Divorce Living Arrangements, Parent Conflict and Long-Term Physical Health Correlates for Children of Divorce," *Journal of Family Psychology* (2007): 21.

p. 94   "Those impacted by divorce are more likely . . . " Ingunn Storksen et al., "Marriages and Psychological Distress Among Adult Offspring of Divorce: A Norwegian Study," *Scandinavian Journal of Psychology* (2007) 49: 467–476.

p. 96   "With notable consistency . . . " M. D. Resnick, P. S. Bearman, R. W. Blum, K. E. Bauman, K. M. Harris, J. Jones et al., "Protecting Adolescents from Harm: Findings from the National Longitudinal Study on Adolescent Health," *JAMA* (1997) 278 (10): 823–32. Also see L. Kann, C. W. Warren, W. A. Harris et al., "Youth Risk Behavior Surveillance—United States, 1995," *Morbidity and Mortality Weekly Report* (1996) 45: 1–84.

p. 96   "Recent scholarship demonstrates . . . " E. R. DeVore and K. R. Ginsburg, "The Protective Effects of Good Parenting on Adolescents," *Current Opinion in Pediatrics* (2005) 17: 460–465.

p. 96   "These differences appeared to be explained . . . " J. F. Klausli and M. T. Owen, "Stable Maternal Cohabitation, Couple Relationship Quality, and Characteristics of the Home Environment in the Child's First Two Years," *Journal of Family Psychology* (2009) 23: 103–106.

p. 97   "Two out of every five . . . " *U.S. News and World Report*, February 27, 1995, 39.

p. 97   "The statistics about the effects of fatherlessness are disturbing. . . ."
         U.S. D.H.H.S. Bureau of the Census.

p. 97   "Girls who grow up without their father . . . " B. J. Ellis, J. E. Bates
         et al., "Does Father Absence Place Daughters at Special Risk for
         Early Sexual Activity and Teenage Pregnancy?" *Child Development*
         (2003) 74: 801–821.

p. 97   "This area of research broadly . . . " See review of literature in
         P. B. Perrin, J. O. Baker et al., "Development, Validation, and
         Confirmatory Factor Analysis of the Father Hunger Scale," *Psychology
         of Men and Masculinity* (2009) 10: 314–327.

p. 97   "Fatherlessness is the most harmful demographic . . . " See D.
         Blankenhorn, *Fatherless America: Confronting Our Most Urgent Social
         Problem* (New York: Basic Books, 1995), and D. Popenoe, *Life
         Without Father* (New York: Free Press, 1996), cited in P. B. Perrin,
         J. O. Baker et al., "Development, Validation, and Confirmatory
         Factor Analysis of the Father Hunger Scale," 315. Originally cited
         in B. M. Erickson, *Longing for Dad: Father Loss and Its Impact*
         (Deerfield Beach, FL: Health Communications, 1998), 68.

p. 98   "For daughters, this sense of need . . . " P. B. Perrin, J. O. Baker et
         al., "Development, Validation, and Confirmatory Factor Analysis
         of the Father Hunger Scale," 314–327.

Chapter 6: Self-Care: Health and Wellness

p. 107   "But the soul is present as a whole . . ." Augustine, *The Immortality
         of the Soul*, 26.25.

p. 107   "The idea that the spirit is merely a function of the brain . . . "
         Warren S. Brown et al., in *Whatever Happened to the Soul? Scientific
         and Theological Portraits of Human Nature* (Minneapolis: Fortress
         Press, 1998), xii, states that "there is, however, no way to provide
         absolute proof that the dualist theories are false."

p. 112   "There is a growing interest in the impact . . . " Michael E.
         McCullough, William T. Hoyt, David B. Larson, Harold G.
         Koenig, Carl Thoresen, "Religious Involvement and Mortality:
         A Meta-Analytic Review," *Health Psychology* (2000) 20: 211–22;
         Michael E. McCullough, Howard S. Friedman, Craig K. Enders,
         Leslie R. Martin, "Does Devoutness Delay Death? Psychological
         Investment in Religion and Its Association with Longevity in the
         Terman Sample," *Journal of Personality and Social Psychology* (2009)
         97 (5): 866–882. See also Daniel Hawes, "Devoutness and Death,"
         Psychology Today 2009 at *www.psychologytoday.com/blog/evolved
         -primate/200911/devoutness-and-death*.

p. 112   "In the many studies reviewed in the Oxford University Press *Handbook . . .*" H. G. Koenig, M. E. McCullough, D. B. Larson, *Handbook of Religion and Health* (New York: Oxford University Press, 2001).

p. 112   "Weekly attendance at religious services . . . " Daniel E. Hall, "Religious Attendance: More Cost-Effective Than Lipitor?" *Journal of the American Board of Family Medicine* (2006) 19: 103–109.

pp. 112–113 "In spite of all the enforced physical . . . " Viktor Frankl, *Man's Search for Meaning* (New York: Washington Square Press, 1959), 55–57.

p. 114   "Only about a third of these people seek treatment . . . " *www.who .int/mentalhealth/management/depression/definition/en.*

p. 114   "Effective treatments include several kinds of therapy." Anthony Roth and Peter Fonagy, *What Works for Whom? Second Edition: A Critical Review of Psychotherapy Research* (New York: Guilford Press, 2005), 78; D. R. Hopko, C. W. Lejuez, J. P. Lepage, S. D. Hopko, D. W. McNeil, "A Brief Behavioral Activation Treatment for Depression," *Behavior Modification* (2004) 27: 458–469.

p. 114   "Medication has also been shown to be effective . . . " I. Kirsch, B. J. Deacon, T. B. Huedo-Medina, A. Scoboria, T. J. Moore, B. T. Johnson, "Initial Severity and Antidepressant Benefits: A Meta-Analysis of Data Submitted to the Food and Drug Administration," *Public Library of Science Medicine* (2008) 2: 45; E. H. Turner, A. M. Matthews, E. Linardatos, R. A. Tell, R. Rosenthal, "Selective Publication of Antidepressant Trials and Its Influence on Apparent Efficacy," *New England Journal of Medicine* (2008) 358 (3): 252–260.

p. 114   "A combination of therapy and medication . . . " Benjamin W. Van Voorhees, et al., "Treat Depressed Teens with Medication and Psychotherapy," *Journal of Family Practice* (2008) 57 (11): 735–739.

p. 116   "The use of some fertilizers . . . " See Buck Levin, PhD, RD, *Environmental Nutrition: Understanding the Link between Environment, Food Quality, and Disease* (Vashon Island, WA: Hinge Pin, 1999).

p. 117   "Beyond this, God expected his people . . . " See Jordan Rubin, *The Great Physician's Rx for Health and Wellness: Seven Keys to Unlock Your Health Potential* (Nashville: Nelson Books, 2005).

Chapter 7: Sleep and Sabbath Rest

p. 121   "Sleep appears to play a role . . . " D. T. Max, "The Secrets of Sleep," *National Geographic* (May 2010): 75–93.

p. 121   "... approximately 29 percent of U.S. adults..." C. A. Schoenborn and P. F. Adams, "Sleep duration as a correlate of smoking, alcohol-use, leisure-time physical inactivity, and obesity among adults: United States, 2004–2006." Available at *www.cdc.gov/nchs/data/hestat/sleep04–06/sleep04–06.pdf.*

p. 121   "... 70 percent of those surveyed reported..." CDC, "Public health surveillance for behavioral risk factors in a changing environment: recommendations from the Behavioral Risk Factor Surveillance Team," *Morbidity and Mortality Weekly Report* (2003) 52 (No. RR-9).

p. 121   "... increased risk for heart disease," Michelle Cardi et al., "Health Behavior Risk Factors Across Age as Predictors of Cardiovascular Disease Diagnosis," *Journal of Aging & Health* (2010) 22 (5): 759–775.

p. 121   "type 2 diabetes" D. J. Gottlieb, N. M. Punjabi, A. B. Newman et al., "Association of Sleep Time with Diabetes Mellitus and Impaired Glucose Tolerance," *Archives of Internal Medicine* 165 (8): 863–867.

p. 121   "mental illness, including psychosis," F. S. Goes, P. P. Zandi, K. Miao K., et al., "Mood-incongruent psychotic features in bipolar disorder: familial aggregation and suggestive linkage to 2p11-q14 and 13q21–33," *American Journal of Psychiatry* (2007) 164 (2): 236–47; S. Banks and D. F. Dinges, "Behavioral and Physiological Consequences of Sleep Restriction," *Journal of Clinical Sleep Medicine* (2007) 3: 519–28.

p. 121   "damage to the brain," Jerome M. Siegel, "Why We Sleep," *Scientific American, www.semel.ucla.edu/sleepresearch/sciam2003/sciamsleep.pdf.*

p. 121   "decreased ability to heal wounds." A. N. Vgontzas, G. Mastorakos, E. O. Bixler, A. Kales, P. W. Gold, G. P. Chrousos, "Sleep deprivation effects on the activity of the hypothalamic-pituitary-adrenal and growth axes: potential clinical implications," *Clinical Endocrinology* (1999) 51 (2): 205–15; L. Mostaghimi, W. H. Obermeyer, B. Ballamudi, D. Martinez-Gonzalez, R. M. Benca, "Effects of Sleep Deprivation on Wound Healing," *Journal of Sleep Research* (2005) 14 (3): 213.

p. 121   "Consider a relaxing routine..." "Too Early to Get Up, Too Late to Get Back to Sleep," *Harvard Women's Health Watch* (2010) 17: 1–3.

pp. 125–126 "The child cannot allow himself..." Ernest Becker, *The Denial of Death* (New York: The Free Press, 1973), 3–4.

p. 127   "When we're stressed out, we are often unable to focus . . ." *www.webmd* *.com/balance/stress-management/stress-management-effects-of-stress.*

p. 127   "But we can learn again to relax." Herbert Benson, MD, *The Relaxation Response* (New York: HarperCollins, 1975).

p. 130   "The powerful healing effects of being alone . . . " P. Suedfeld, "The Benefits of Boredom: Sensory Deprivation Reconsidered," *American Scientist* 63 (1975): 60–69; and *Loneliness: A Sourcebook for Current Theory, Research, and Therapy*, eds. L. A. Peplau and D. Perlman (New York: Wiley, 1982).

pp. 130–131 ". . . the story of John Kavanaugh . . . " Brennan Manning, *Ruthless Trust: The Ragamuffin's Path to God* (New York: HarperCollins, 2000), 5.

p. 131   ". . . the kingdom of God is here and now." See Carlson, *You Were Made for Love,* 216.

p. 132   "How misleading is the theory . . . " Lewis Sperry Chafer, *He That Is Spiritual* (Grand Rapids: Zondervan, 1967), 60–61.

p. 133   "Joy, which was the small publicity of the pagan . . . " G. K. Chesterton, *Orthodoxy* (Garden City, NY: Image Books, 1959), 160.

Chapter 8: Stewardship

p. 138   "One expressed the opinion that the Christian worldview . . . " Francis A. Schaeffer, *Pollution and the Death of Man: The Christian View of Ecology* (Wheaton, IL: Tyndale House, 1970), 12–14.

pp. 138–139 "Near the end of his life, Darwin . . . " Schaeffer, *Pollution,* 11–14.

p. 139   "It was then that I realized what a horrible situation this was." Schaeffer, *Pollution,* 42.

p. 140   "Earth contains earthquakes . . . " Steven Schafersman, PhD, "Happy Darwin Day!" *www.texscience.org/reviews/darwin-day.htm*

p. 140   "Atheism is nothing more than the noises reasonable people make . . . " Sam Harris, *Letter to a Christian Nation* (New York: Alfred A. Knopf, 2006), 51–52.

p. 141   "Kindness is the law of the universe . . . " Charles H. Spurgeon, *The Treasury of David, Psalm 145:9. www.spurgeon.org/treasury/ ps145.htm.*

p. 141   ". . . finds no real difference between a human and a pig . . . " Peter Singer, *Writings on an Ethical Life* (New York: HarperCollins, 2000), 136–139.

p. 142   "Richard Dawkins has called pantheism 'a sexed-up atheism.' "
         Ross Douthat, *New York Times,* December 21, 2009.

p. 143   "Christians reject the view that there is no distinction . . . " Schaeffer,
         Pollution, 49–51.

p. 144   ". . . a reason for dealing with each created thing . . . " Schaeffer,
         Pollution, 55.

p. 146   "The duty of kindness to animals . . . " Spurgeon, *The Treasury of
         David, Psalm 145:9.*

p. 150   "Farming practices that don't allow for . . . " *www.agroforestry.net/
         overstory/overstory42.html*

Chapter 9: Creation and the Goal of History

p. 155   "The universe has a design . . ." From Stephen Hawking and Leonard
         Mlodinow, *The Grand Design* (New York: Bantam Books, 2010),
         187.

p. 157   "The things that began to happen . . . " C. S. Lewis, *The Last Battle*
         (New York: HarperTrophy, 1994), 228.

p. 159   "I believe that the kingdom of God was brought into that room . . . "
         See Carlson, *You Were Made for Love,* 231–232.

p. 160   "A Christian-based science and technology . . . " Schaeffer, *Pollution,*
         81.

p. 161   "But let's at least acknowledge that a part of our responsibility . . . "
         Wendell Berry, *Another Turn of the Crank* (Washington, DC:
         Counterpoint, 1995).

p. 162   "I've done this for several years now . . . " Kenneth V. Lundberg, "I
         Worried So Much About World Hunger Today that I Went Home
         and Ate Five Cookies," *His* magazine, April 1984, 22–23.

Epilogue: The Importance of Purpose and Meaning

p. 163   "Maturity requires . . . a clear comprehension of life's pur-
         pose . . . " G. W. Allport. *www.religion-online.org/showchapter
         .asp?title=1900&C=1714.*

p. 164   "He later would ask suicidal patients . . . " Frankl, *Man's Search for
         Meaning,* ix, 81ff., 103.

p. 169   "the worm at the core" William James, *Varieties of Religious Experience:
         A Study in Human Nature* (New York: Mentor Edition, 1958),
         281.

p. 171   "Your world (in the womb) is dark, safe, secure." Philip Yancey, *Where Is God When It Hurts?* (Grand Rapids: Zondervan, 1977), 179–180.

p. 172   "Gordon W. Allport raises the possibility . . . " According to Allport, this may be done by seeing oneself as a communist, a pacifist, a humanist, or a Christian, etc. . . . providing a value-orientation that brings a sense of unity in life. Salman Rushdie, for example, appealed to the Muslim community for understanding in his book *Midnight's Children*: "Life without God seems to believers to be an idiocy, pointless, beneath contempt. It does not seem so to non-believers. To accept that the world, here, is all there is; to go through it, toward and into death, without the consolations of religion seems, well, at least as courageous and rigorous to us as the espousal of faith seems to you. Secularism and its works deserve your respect, not your contempt." The point that must be understood is that within this philosophical framework, Rushdie, like each of us, is seeking to discover a way to make some sense of life, a way to understand the way things are. Even though such an approach to life provides no reasons for an ultimate sense of meaning, it appears to provide for its adherents some "immediate" meaning.

p. 173   "Jonathan Edwards endeavored to describe . . . " Jonathan Edwards, *Religious Affections* (Portland, OR: Multnomah Press, 1984), 10.

p. 174   ". . . a variety of studies suggesting the positive impact of living with purpose . . . " Patrick E. McKnight and Todd B. Kashdan, "Purpose in Life as a System That Creates and Sustains Health and Well-Being: An Integrative, Testable Theory," *Review of General Psychology* 13 (2009).

p. 174   "Psychologist Erik Erikson describes stages of psychosocial development . . ." Erik Erikson, *Identity and Life Cycle* (New York: W. W. Gorton & Co., 1980), 129.

p. 176   "The great perplexity of our time . . . " Ernest Becker, *Denial*, 6.

pp. 177–178 "The matter is quite simple. The Bible is very easy to understand." Søren Kierkegaard, *Provocative Spiritual Writings of Kierkegaard,* compiled and edited by Charles E. Moore (Farmington, PA: Plough, 2002), 201.